Second Order Project Management

For Marjorie

Second Order Project Management

MICHAEL CAVANAGH

GOWER

Published by
Gower Publishing Limited
Wey Court East
Union Road
Farnham
Surrey, GU9 7PT
England

Gower Publishing Company
Suite 420
101 Cherry Street
Burlington
VT 05401-4405
USA

www.gowerpublishing.com

Michael Cavanagh has asserted his moral right under the Copyright, Designs and Patents Act, 1988, to be identified as the author of this work.

British Library Cataloguing in Publication Data
Cavanagh, Michael.
    Second order project management. – (Advances in project management)
    1. Project management.
    I. Title II. Series
    658.4'04 – dc22

Library of Congress Cataloging-in-Publication Data
Cavanagh, Michael, 1949–
    Second order project management / by Michael Cavanagh.
        p. cm. – (Advances in project management)
    Includes bibliographical references and index.
    ISBN 978-1-4094-1094-2 (hardback : alk. paper) – ISBN 978-1-4094-1095-9 (ebook)
    1. Project management. 2. Project management – Methodology. 3. Technological complexity. I. Title.

    HD69.P75C384 2011
    658.4'04 – dc23

                                                                              2011027142

ISBN 9781409410942 (pbk)
ISBN 9781409410959 (ebk)

Printed and bound in Great Britain by the
MPG Books Group, UK

CONTENTS

LIST OF FIGURES AND MUSIC EXAMPLES

FIGURES

MUSIC EXAMPLES

ABOUT THE AUTHOR

Michael Cavanagh is a consultant specialising in organisational learning, development and project management. In his 40-year career, Michael Cavanagh has worked as a Programmer, Systems Analyst, Project Manager, Department Head and Consultant in a number of business sectors. In recent years, he has concentrated on the transfer of knowledge and wisdom in an organisational context. This work on experiential learning has led to the focus of his research and consulting activity being the use of systems thinking techniques to perform 'forensic' analysis of major project failure and the ways in which lessons can be derived and corrective process improvement implemented, applying these ideas in very large long-term projects

Michael has worked alongside many organisations in Defence, Transportation and Petrochemical sectors across Europe, the USA, Canada and the Middle East. He is a regular speaker at international conferences and in major Business Schools.

Michael is also an ordained Anglican priest in the Church of Ireland, responsible for the churches of the Kenmare and Dromod Union, Co. Kerry.

AUTHOR'S NOTE

It's probably a good idea to start by saying what this book is not. Although it makes some points that I passionately feel need to be made if the Project Management (PM) profession is to advance, it is not simply a polemic. Neither is it a textbook or definitive guide to Second Order PM tools and techniques, although I have included descriptions of some which I have found both usable and useful in my own practice.

What I hope it *is*, is what is sometimes called a rock in the pond – an attempt to perturb the existing PM canon to see what splashes out. I hope it will be read by Project Managers themselves, the best of whom are always curious and keen to improve their own practice; and to them I hereby give permission to disagree profoundly with anything I say which doesn't ring true in their own experience ... provided they, just for a minute, consider that they might be wrong and I might possibly be right. (And should you then still disagree, let me know and I shall afford you the same respect.)

I also hope that Project Managers will buy more than one copy – because the main incentive to write, and the outcome I am looking for, is to help alleviate the frustration that every member of the profession has experienced when trying to gain approval for investment in process improvement, from sponsors whose background and discipline doesn't equip them to understand enough about the subject to have the confidence that would justify a 'yes'.

So ... buy copies for the Board. Read it with them. (Or *to* them!) Talk to them about the issues. Cherry-pick. Experiment on a small project. Measure the results using *meaningful* metrics, but don't measure until the change has got to a steady state (too many process improvements get abandoned because they haven't been given time to get past the learning curve).

And then share what you discover,'cos we're in this together, and we can learn much from each other, if we so choose.

Michael C.

michael.cavanagh@eircom.net

FOREWORD

As we move quickly into the twenty-first century we can see clear evidence that the number and size of complex projects is increasing. Just as evident, and supported by countless reviews by bodies such as the UK National Audit Office and the US Government Accountability Office, is that, whilst necessary, our classical approach to Project Management is not in itself sufficient.

Regardless of your lens or worldview, complex projects are by their very nature neither deterministic nor predictable. They require us to reframe or expand the set of tools, methods and techniques used to deliver successful outcomes in complex environments

Key to successful outcomes is new, more developed thinking flowing from complexity science and real-world experience. But thought alone is not enough – we need to move beyond the significant theoretical advances in complexity to enable its practical application to complex projects and the management of complexity. As an Associate of the International Centre for Complex Project Management, Michael Cavanagh is one of a small number of individuals who have taken a leadership position in addressing this challenge with the publishing of this book.

Michael's work begins by looking at Complexity and Complexity drivers, suggests a Project Complexity Measure and introduces the need for 'second order' tools, methods and techniques. Second Order PM has a number of components including the 'Systems Approach', 'Experiential Learning' and 'Appropriate Contracting'. Outlining the components of Second Order PM, Michael emphasises that on their own they are insufficient and must be supported by 'Improvisational Leadership', 'Outcome Management' and 'Ethical' considerations. The remainder of Part I gives detailed consideration to these enablers. Part II focuses on providing some answers by detailing a number of theories and practical techniques for improving complex Project Management delivery.

Well done on a refreshing approach to the challenge presented by complex projects. For the reader, if you are looking to develop your thinking and tool set beyond classical or Second Order Project Management with a succinct and easily understood read then I commend this book to you.

Stephen Hayes MBE
CEO International Centre for Complex Project Management

ACKNOWLEDGEMENTS

There are many people who, consciously or unconsciously, have contributed to the thoughts and production of this little book.

Jonathan Norman from Gower; Prof. Darren Dalcher from the National Centre for Project Management; Stephen Hayes, Jo Spencer and their ICCPM partners; Tim Cummins from IACCM; Mary McKinlay from APM; Profs. Bob Wood and Trevor Wood-Harper from the University of Salford (where we did the real work) and other places; Patrick Hoverstadt from Fractal Consulting; Pauline Marsh, Rob Sneddon and Frank Rainford from BAE Systems; Manfred Saynisch, who first coined the term 'Second Order' and who continues to work to promote thinking and develop support material in this field; Rob Fordham from Presto for writing the 'complex' music (now finish the whole piece!); and Manchester City Football Club, whose unpredictability makes supporting them an incredibly frustrating and complex project.

All the interviewees and past colleagues who have informed the discussion, speaking from their personal experience: in particular Terry Cooke-Davies; Sergey Bushuyev; Ed Hoffman; Alan Lamond; Christophe Bredillet; Tim Banfield; Gary Marsh; Peter Fielder and Tim Cummins. I hope I conveyed your meaning accurately – if not, mea maxima culpa.

And of course, love and thanks to my family; and my saviour, redeemer and friend, the Lord Jesus Christ.

Michael Cavanagh
St Patrick's Rectory, Kenmare, Co. Kerry

INTRODUCTION

THE CHALLENGE OF COMPLEX PROJECTS

> *We choose to go to the moon. We choose to go to the moon in this decade and do the other things, not because they are easy, but because they are hard, because that goal will serve to organize and measure the best of our energies and skills, because that challenge is one that we are willing to accept, one we are unwilling to postpone, and one which we intend to win, and the others, too.*
> *President John F. Kennedy, Rice University, September 12, 1962*

And win they did. Despite the technical difficulties, a man took a small step, mankind a giant leap. Could it happen today? The 'science' of Project Management (PM) has progressed hugely in the ensuing 50 years – we have a bagful of well-developed methods and tools, and a pretty much comprehensive Project Management Body of Knowledge.

Ironically, these things are probably why we would never leave the ground. Necessary, yes – but they aren't enough, and relying on them alone won't work. 'Scientific' management relies on the precise definition of the task in hand. The bigger and more complex a project gets, the more imprecise that definition. Dealing with uncertainty demands flexibility, and the tenacity to deliver in the face of unknown obstacles and difficulties.

If today's President of the USA stood at that same podium, and announced that the nation has chosen to eliminate AIDS, to help successfully rebuild a war-torn nation, to combat global warming or to go to Mars before the end of the next decade – certainly complex tasks, but no less technically achievable than a lunar landing – it would not be science that would deliver the promise. It would be resolute leadership, wisdom, diplomacy and most of all an accommodated understanding that, whatever the cost, the outcome would be worth it.

The cynics of the world would laugh anyway – citing any number of high-profile project failures, where costs and schedules have been exceeded by orders of magnitude. As an example (but only the most recent example of many), the 2009 Gray report on the UK Ministry of Defence (MoD) suggested that defence equipment programmes on average experience a schedule overrun of 80 per cent and cost 40 per cent more than planned. The surprising aspect of this report was that no one was surprised. It appears that poor project performance on complex programmes is inevitable. So should we do only the easy things, even if the hard things are what we need? I don't think so. That's not the way we make progress.

While it is inarguable that many complex projects have indeed overrun and underdelivered – it is *profoundly* untrue that this is an inevitable outcome. Rather, it is simply the case that the prevailing acquisition environment militates towards failure. It is unrealistic to depend on toolsets and skillsets that may be adequate for simple projects but cannot cope with complexity. They might work sometimes – but their success has probably owed more to individual heroism and the conjunctions of the planets than the suitability of the processes deployed. If you do what you've always done, you'll get what you've always got, and if what you've always got isn't good enough, you need to do something else. Simply applying the same PM processes more rigorously (the most common approach) is like shouting louder when a person from another country doesn't understand English. Albert Einstein: '*Insanity is doing the same thing and expecting different results.*'

In the face of complexity, we thus need to do different things, and there are four major issues to address; the Conspiracy of Optimism (CoO), the use of Appropriate Contracting models, the application of methods and tools which are capable of dealing with complexity, and above all, the need for flexible, creative, inspirational leadership behaviours. Together, these constitute what we term Second Order PM, and they are summarised below.

A *CoO* exists across the supply chain. *'Pessimists don't get programmes.'* Purchasers have to market their favoured project to their sponsors to gain the approvals they need, and adopt a mindset ready to believe the lowest compliant bidder in order to gain that acceptance. Using competition as a bargaining tool (weapon might be a better word), they will strive to drive price down, even though deep in their hearts they know this is unlikely to be what they will eventually pay. On the other hand, suppliers accept that in a competitive environment, building adequate risk into their bid is likely to make them too expensive; so they will tend to say what their customer wants to hear, knowing that scope creep will allow them an excuse to increase the final price. Neither party really trusts the other, since both have been enculturalised to a combative procurement scenario; deep down they both know what's going on, but they won't (can't) admit it to each other or themselves.

Aggressive media pressure on government agencies, the reluctance of both politicians and CEOs to invest strategically (with the benefits of such investment being delivered not to themselves, but their successors); the demand for short-term results from corporate shareholders in the competitive theatres of defence, construction and other major public sector programmes; all these work against the ideal of an honest, open, mutually trusting engagement between stakeholders and the agreement of *Appropriate Contracting Models*. Again, all parties are aware of this – but can't afford to be the first to admit it and sign pragmatic contracts that allow for unknowns and uncertainties. A flexible agreement based on mutual trust would be contrary to accepted negotiation tactics, which are intrinsically a philosophy of *'You show me yours, and I'll show you mine – but you have to show me yours first.'*

There is a huge amount of empirical evidence proving that even the best estimation techniques will only be accurate within a 25 per cent cone of uncertainty, *even when detailed requirements have been agreed* – and yet contracts are let, often on a fixed price basis, far too early in the project lifecycle. Whilst concentrating on software, Barry Boehm's *Software Engineering Economics* (1981) gives a strong argument illustrating this which can be extrapolated to other engineering disciplines. Hugely wasteful effort is often expended on attempting to deliver to initial estimates, rather than admit the impossibility of accurately predicting unknown unknowns. The issue is exponentially exacerbated in proportion to project complexity.

Similarly, contracts with an emphasis on punitive measures for non-performance of the supplier (though rarely matched by equally-weighted sanctions for non-performance of the customer!) are generally counterproductive. There is nothing wrong in using the threat of sanctions as a contractual incentive, but these have to be realistic, with an equitable balance between delivery/reward and shared risk, if the outcome is not to be a combination of poor product performance, unsatisfied customers and financial penalties on the supplier.

Complex PM Competencies and Tools are not just a question of more rigorous application of existing 'Industry Standard' methods and techniques, which is the equivalent of shouting louder to make a foreigner understand what you're saying. People are *never* incompetent on purpose – but if they are unaware of the existence of anything better, they will use what they have. Unfortunately, the competencies required to manage high degrees of complexity are not usually found on Engineering or PM curricula – and it may even be that they demand different personal attributes to those commonly found in people proficient in the 'science' of those disciplines.

These skills encompass aspects of behaviour as well as competence. Certainly, the PM repertoire, especially in the areas of System Thinking and Experiential Learning, needs to be developed and implemented. But of equal importance is the need for behavioural skills to evolve to meet the challenges of increasingly complex activity and its related uncertainty. Complex PM demands vision and motivation; empathy; attention to relationship building, in order that trust may be mutually awarded and maintained though difficult periods; the ability to take a systemic (holistic) view; consummate communication skills; practical application of experientially-derived wisdom; and perhaps most of all, courage – the courage to be able to speak the truth (and hear it!), and to take good risk. The potential energy of an unexploded bomb helps, too – Theodore Roosevelt: '*Speak softly and carry a big stick; you will go far.*' We should emphasise 'unexploded' – bombast and bullying rarely work more than once.

But above all, although all these factors are critical to complex project success, it is *Leadership* that is paramount. John Kennedy didn't hand over a set of detailed requirements, but a vision that everyone could share, allowing them to relate the task in hand to the wider goal. Strong leadership inspires and motivates a set of disparate individuals with specialist expertise and domain knowledge; it institutionalises a common value set across the entire community, who understand and accept that their individual tasks are not ends in themselves, but contributions to a bigger purpose.

In the end, it's all about outcome. Projects don't end at the implementation phase – they continue throughout the lifetime of the product, and the true measures of their success will be the usefulness, durability and beauty of what they have delivered. No one remembers the budget or schedule overruns of the Pyramids, the Taj Mahal or Sydney Opera House. No one cares, either.

There are many calls upon leadership attention, many different stakeholders to be convinced, many cultural and behavioural changes needed if the above issues are to be addressed. Not least, a grown-up attitude to project complexity demands the absolute necessity of sacrificing short-term gain in order to deliver programmes of long-term organisational, social and international importance. The best of the best of the worldwide PM community understand this, which is why they have combined under the auspice of the International Centre for Complex Project Management (ICCPM) to guide research and implement the necessary competencies and process changes within their own discipline, but in itself that will not be enough.

Prophets, unfortunately, have no honour in their own country. Until their message is heard *and acted upon* by the senior executive in both public and private sectors, who alone possess sufficient power to invest, support and lead a permanent behavioural change in Complex Project Acquisition, we shall stay on Earth forever.

PART I

UNCERTAINTY, COMPLEXITY AND IMPACT ON PROJECTS

CHAPTER 1

WHAT MAKES PROJECTS COMPLEX?

Some problems are so complex that you have to be highly intelligent and well informed just to be undecided about them.

Dr Laurence J. Peter

Let's begin by understanding what 'complex' means in project terms – and the easiest way to do this is to start with what it isn't. Clearly, complexity isn't *simple*; but neither is it *complicated*. The difference is in the degree of uncertainty. Complicated things are difficult to produce; they are usually made up of a large number of components; they may take a long time to build – but they *are* capable of being described in detail, down to the last brick, rivet or connection. Because of that, their design and construction can be accurately and precisely articulated and planned; they can be built even by people who don't fully understand what they are doing, so long as they comply – to the letter – with the engineering processes that are laid down by those who do. Any failure is due to either lack of compliance or an inadequacy in the process description.

I tried to build a kit car once – a Westfield Speedsport – and got stuck at a very early stage. The salesman claimed that it would take 150 hours to build. What he meant was that it would take someone who knew what they were doing 150 hours. After 150 *weeks*, I gave up and got some expert help. In my (admittedly rather pathetic) defence, I submit that the reason I ended up having to get outside assistance lies at the feet of the author of the build manual, who clearly didn't understand just how great was my lack of understanding of even the first principles of mechanical engineering. Putting the car together wasn't a complex task – it was just complicated. Given a set of instructions at my level of experience and previous knowledge, I could have built it on my own. I think.

Complexity arises when a design or a plan contains unknowns and uncertainties. Although it may very well be broadly accurate, it will almost certainly be precisely wrong. The real reason it took me years instead of hours to build the car wasn't only how complicated were the nuts, bolts and wiring – it was the external elements that I hadn't bargained for, the main one being the million and one unpredicted distractions and a failure to realise how unpleasant and demotivating it would be to work in an unheated garage. This was actually the worst kind of complexity – it's bad enough if the uncertainties are expected (*'known unknowns'* to use a Rumsfeldism). When the unknowns are unknown (*'things we don't know we don't know'*), and therefore unacknowledged, there could be a few surprises in store ...

To an extent, then, every project – indeed every future venture – has its element of complexity, since we live in a constantly changing world. (viz. Heraclitus of Ephesus – *'you can't stand in the same river twice'*) No one can predict the changes in the external 'PEST' (Political, Economic. Social, Technological) environment with 100 per cent certainty. In the simplest projects, such changes are unlikely to have much effect; but the level of project complexity grows in direct proportion to the number of areas of uncertainty, and there is a point at which possible changes in both the external environment and the capability of the internal organisation demand that the level of complexity is identified and addressed. We term these areas of uncertainty 'Complexity Drivers' – not all of which affect every project to the same extent. They comprise any element of the project that interacts with its environment and other components, whether these be people, organisations, technologies and/or processes. The Project Complexity Measure (PCM) will thus be the combination of any given project's Complexity Drivers, their depth, the number of interactions between them, and the organisational capability to deal with these.

If complex projects are to be successfully planned and managed, it therefore becomes necessary (and in my opinion should be mandatory) to perform a PCM Assessment (essentially an additional component of a pre-project risk identification phase) at the earliest stages of the project lifecycle, and to maintain the currency of this assessment throughout.

There are two Complexity Driver dimensions.

Capability drivers are relevant to the organisation and the individuals who make up the project team, and will include:

- leadership style/experience and behavioural attributes such as wisdom, action orientation, inspiration, focus, courage, ability to influence;
- team experience, structure and track record;
- platform/technology novelty;
- learning culture; flexibility and creativity;
- Risk aversity/risk seeking organisational culture;
- internal and external environmental turbulence;
- process/method/tool experience.

Project-specific drivers are made up of elements such as:

- urgency/business criticality;
- outcome novelty;
- intricacy;
- scope, cost/budget, duration;
- safety criticality;
- requirements maturity and stability;
- stakeholder numbers/geographical separation;
- stakeholder organisational stability;
- external regulation/governance;
- platform/technology interactions;
- number of component (subsystem and stakeholder) interactions and relationships;
- contracting models.

An expanded description of a PCM Assessment process, and the generic assessment questionnaire, can be found on the authors website www.mcavanagh.com.

As complexity increases in respect of either or both of the above types of driver, so the necessary response must also change; and this introduces the concept of 'first' and 'second' order tools, methods and techniques. The appropriate responses can best be illustrated by means of placing them on a Complexity Assessment Matrix, as in Figure 1.1.

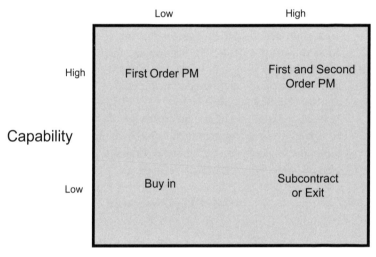

Figure 1.1   Complexity Assessment Matrix

Low Experience, Low Complexity – An example of which could be any 'Black Box' component such as 'Plug-and Play' software, where the complexity and experience all lie with the provider and all the end user has to do is load a CD or connect an interface. If an organisation were even to contemplate building such a product for themselves, it would not only be a culpable waste of money, but would also result in a sub-standard product (though it has been tried, with risible results!).

High Experience, Low Complexity – These are the routine, bread and butter, cash cow products – possibly tailored to individual customer preference, but essentially standardised. Projects in this domain will have been successfully executed many times before (and they may in fact be 'complicated') but the performance of the deliverable will be known and proven. However, that does not mean that they should be allowed to run outside a controlled project framework. They still demand rigorous application of what we shall term 'First Order' PM tools such as Earned Value Management, Lifecycle Management and Gateway Reviews, alongside PRINCE 2, CMM-I and similar 'process' guidelines. The quality of the delivered product or service will be a function of process compliance and competent management.

Low Experience, High Complexity – This is where things begin to get difficult, and the 'can-do' organisation is in danger of biting off more than it can chew. It takes courage to admit that a project is too complex for the existing team experience level to undertake – but that is where real leadership kicks in, over and above simple management tasks. It may be that herein lies the strongest argument for PCM Assessment – the danger lies in a lack of appreciation of the true complexity of the task, and this is likely to be most strongly the case where the project-at-hand is novel to the organisation. All too often, however, the assessment is not performed, and uninformed commitments are made out of eagerness to please, enthusiasm to get going and a reluctance to spend time and money on an exercise that may eventually prove not to have been needed. It is worth quoting Admiral Chester Nimitz, C-in-C Pacific, in evidence to the Court of Enquiry on the 1944 typhoon which resulted in the loss of three ships and almost 800 officers and men: '*The time for taking all measures for a ship's safety is while still able to do so. Nothing is more dangerous that for a seaman to be grudging in taking precautions lest they turn out to be unnecessary. Safety at Sea for a thousand years has depended on exactly the opposite philosophy.*' Projects in this quadrant are the ones that make the headlines when they, almost inevitably, go wrong.

At an extreme level, the correct response is to get out quick. Where this is not possible, for whatever reason (political or commercial pressure being the most usual), then it becomes imperative to acquire the necessary experience from outside the team, either through recruitment (unlikely to be quick enough) or external consultancy. This does not mean that the project can simply sit back and watch – unless the consultancy intervention incorporates a managed knowledge/skill/ wisdom transfer, the situation won't improve and next time will be no better. Opportunities for developing internal repertoire must be grasped when they arrive, so that the sum of team experience/repertoire is increased and future projects placed in the top right quadrant.

High Experience, High Complexity – This is where the glittering prizes lie for those individuals and organisations who possess the repertoire and experience to dare to undertake complex tasks – not without risk, but with eyes wide open to the expectation that the unexpected is inevitable. In addition to their mastery and deployment of first order tools and techniques, they place huge importance in operating at a second order level.

So what is Second Order PM? And how does it differ from First Order PM? Can it be performed by the same people?

FIRST AND SECOND ORDER PROJECT MANAGEMENT

*They don't want scales ... they want ... music ... all the scales,
all mixed up ... all the little black notes ... all... piggly-higgly ...
not only that ... they want me to play without **looking** at the little
black notes ... just play!*

Signor Piginini

Example 2.1 Scales and arpeggios

Jim Henson's *The Ghost of Faffner Hall* has an episode entitled 'Music
is more than technique', which includes a scene where the virtuoso
violinist Piginini is discovered in the concert hall basement by the janitor
(who looks suspiciously like Ry Cooder, and ensures a happy ending by
teaching him how to play the blues). The maestro is frightened of going
out in front of his audience, because, although technically brilliant, he
can only play scales and arpeggios, and needs the manuscript in front of
him – but the paying customers want him to play *music*.

Example 2.2 Excerpt from 'The Flow of the Nile'
© Rob Fordham. Used with permission.

As anyone who has ever tried seriously to learn to play an instrument will testify, scales and arpeggios are hugely important – they provide the foundation of the technique necessary to make progress beyond an intermediate level. In themselves, however, they would never pass the 'Old Grey Whistle Test' – and no one would ever buy a ticket to hear them. Essentially, they are the 'good practice' processes that every musician needs to master, and then to apply appropriately in order to convey the message and emotion of the music. They are adequate for simple tunes – however a concert-level performance requires a different skillset altogether – not replacing, but *in addition to*, the basic principles.

So it is with PM. The first order tools and techniques – Earned Value Management, PRINCE 2, CMM-I and the rest – are absolutely vital; and up to a certain level of complexity, are quite good enough to do the job and deliver against a firm requirement. As the complexity increases, though, simply following the rules isn't enough. The Project Manager needs to be able to adapt, modify, and improvise, applying first order tools to the specifics of the task at hand (sometimes even 'breaking' their rules on purpose); and in addition, deploy a range of additional, less prescriptive, techniques and methods as and when needed. We call these 'second order'; and where first order tools are designed to apply process rigour, the common element of second order methods is that they are targeted towards the achievement of the deliverable purpose. The term itself was initially coined by Manfred Saynisch as a result of assiduous research over a number of years – his recent papers offer a comprehensive and detailed review of his findings. (Saynisch 2010a; 2010b).

Put another way, it could be argued that first order is about doing things the right way; and second order is about doing the right thing. It may very well be that the behaviours necessary to apply first order methods – attention to detail, rigorous adherence to process – may be a barrier to second order management, in which creativity and lateral thought are major components.

Clearly, it is by far the best policy to attempt to achieve both; but it is equally evident that it is much better to produce the right thing – even if 'playing by ear' – sometimes perhaps doing things the 'wrong' way (albeit inefficiently and at greater cost) – than it is to slavishly follow process but produce something that is less than 100 per cent fit for its intended purpose. Failure to deploy either results in a project being a game of chance – and in the long run, the house always wins. See Figure 2.1. The greater the complexity, the greater the stake.

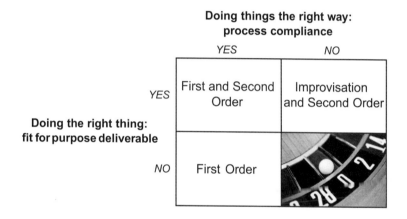

Figure 2.1   Doing the right thing/doing things the right way

There are a number of components of Second Order PM.

The *Systems Approach*, in the sense we use it here, is the deployment of systems thinking and cybernetic concepts to understand the interconnectedness of the deliverable to its subsystems and supersystem and their respective purposes.

Experiential Learning is the means by which both individuals and the organisation can capture, understand, document, disseminate and apply the lessons learnt from both past and current activity.

Appropriate Contracting is the recognition by all stakeholders that in an uncertain future, it is impossible to share risk equitably within a fixed contractual agreement.

On their own, though, even these are insufficient. They depend on *Improvisational (or 'Adhocratic') Leadership* – having the repertoire and courage to pursue the desired outcome in the face of uncertainty and 'events'; and on a project culture of *Outcome Management* (as opposed to Requirements Management), ensuring that there is a mutual accommodation between all stakeholders as to what would constitute fitness for purpose in the through-life operational environment. In addition to this, it is impossible to ignore *ethical* considerations relating to product/service development and implementation.

It helps to start with the issues that leadership must confront.

CHAPTER 3

LEADERSHIP IN AN UNCERTAIN WORLD

*Nine tenths of tactics are certain, and taught in books; but the
irrational tenth is like the kingfisher flashing across the pool, and
that is the test of generals.*

T. E. Lawrence

VISIONS

The bookshelves groan with leadership titles. An Internet search
brings forth literally hundreds of quotes. This is not the place to add
to either. Instead, I want to concentrate on those aspects unique to
complex projects which leadership must address in the 'irrational
tenth'; the inevitability of uncertainty; organisational denial, the CoU;
and shared vision. And the greatest of these is shared vision.

Peter Senge's view, in the bestselling *The Fifth Discipline* (1990), is
that an organisation acts in order to bring about '*the future it most
desires*' and that to achieve this demands a '*shared vision*' across the
entire organisation. He quotes examples such as the collective 'I am
Spartacus' scene in Stanley Kubrick's film of the same name, John
Kennedy's 'Man on the moon by the end of the decade' speech and
other similar (but less iconic) vision statements from large modern
organisations. Perhaps the earliest real (and most powerful) example
of these would be Cato the Elder's clarion call to the Roman Senate in
the latter stages of the Punic Wars – 'Carthago Delenda Est' – which
motivated the campaign to the point where Carthage was not just
destroyed but ploughed over, its fields salted and its population sold
into slavery. A true shared vision acts not just as a guide for action, but

as a motivating factor and a test of appropriate action – is what you are doing contributing to the achievement of the vision? If not, stop it.

Senge sees three caveats to this. First a shared vision must not be the result of a one-off exercise, where managers possibly come back from a workshop or suchlike with the feeling that 'We've done that, got our vision statement, and now we can get on with real work' – implying that creating a shared vision statement is a duty to be discharged, a box to tick. This is a sure indicator that in their view day-to-day activity is what is really important; they will be careful to avoid the cracks in the pavement, and will actually be surprised when they walk into the lamppost.

Second, the vision needs to be truly 'shared' rather than imposed – the personal vision of the boss cannot be assumed to be accepted by all – and in fact an imposed or dictated vision may be more likely to meet (possibly subversive) opposition. *When I hear leaders say 'our vision', and I know that they are really describing 'my vision', I recall Mark Twain's words that the official 'we' should be reserved for 'Kings and people with tapeworm'.*

Thirdly, vision should never be seen as a short-term fix to an immediate problem; it is the philosophy, the 'governing idea' of the enterprise, on which its eyes must be fixed; thereby maintaining the energy and commitment over the long term.

In my personal view, a shared vision should always be expressed in the present tense as a statement of current and/or future fact, aspiration or state of mind rather than an objective to be achieved. '*I am Spartacus*'; '*Carthage is destroyed*'; '*Free at last! Free at last! Thank God Almighty, we are free at last!*'

The vision creates the context and motivation for action, and the leader's responsibility is to relate everyday tasks, even at the lowest level, towards its achievement. The polymath social scientist Herbert Simon suggested that this requires 'subgoal identification': '*when the goals of an organisation cannot be connected operationally with actions ... then decisions will be judged against subordinate goals that* **can** *be connected*' (Simon 1997). The larger and more complex the organisation, however, the harder it is to validate this connection. An illustration of this might be the story originally quoted in the rule of St Benedict (and often retold in other scenarios):

> *A traveler came upon a group of three hard-at-work stonemasons, and asked each in turn what he was doing. The first said, 'I am sanding down this block of marble.' The second said, 'I am preparing a foundation.' The third said, 'I am building a cathedral to the glory of God.'*

It would appear that the foreman of the first two had failed to communicate the vision adequately.

When the corporate vision is remote and unclear in the minds of the workforce, they will, as Simon says, be influenced in '*subtle, and not-so-subtle, ways by (their own) interest and power drives*'. In other words, if you don't communicate the vision, people will work towards their own. Their 'rationality' will be 'bounded' by themselves.

RISK HORIZONS

> *The systems that fail are those that rely on the permanency of human nature, and not on its growth and development.*
>
> Oscar Wilde

The only real certainty in this world is its uncertainty. We deal with the continual changes in the river in which we stand through a process of risk management – whether we call it such or not. Again, this is not the place to discuss risk in detail, the topic being *almost* comprehensively covered elsewhere – however I would suggest that there is an additional second order risk management aspect which needs to be considered as project complexity increases: that being the twin concepts of urgency levels and Risk Horizons.

There are a number of different degrees of urgency. *Premature* urgency results in our trying to take risk mitigation action at too early a stage – when not enough is known about the risk scenario for anything but generalised, unfocussed and therefore potentially very wasteful action. *Latent* urgency is the time window during which enough facts are available to decide upon and execute appropriate risk mitigation. *Manifest* urgency is the point within latency when risk is fast becoming an issue but it is still possible for steps to be taken to ensure collision avoidance – however the clock is loudly ticking away those final seconds to disaster.

Beyond this point, you're going to hit the iceberg whatever you do.

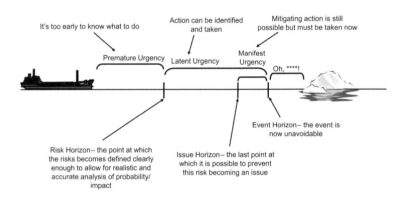

Figure 3.1   The Risk Horizon

Each of these levels is delineated by a horizon. Between premature and latent urgency levels, the Risk Horizon is the point at which risk becomes clearly enough defined to allow for realistic and accurate analysis of probability/impact, with mitigation expenditure being capable of justification and precise targeting. Beyond the Issue Horizon, it will be impossible to prevent the risk becoming an issue unless immediate action is taken – usually at prohibitive cost. At the Event Horizon, the opportunity to mitigate the risk disappears.

The issue is unavoidable. All that can now be done is to attempt to reduce impact. Beyond this point, it may not even be possible to save the crew, even at the expense of the ship.

To assess these levels and horizons accurately demands the application of what Sir Geoffrey Vickers (1965) termed Appreciative Judgement (the combination of reality, value and instrumental judgements) placed alongside a realistic assessment of capabilities and a constant lookout to identify the ever-changing icebergs of a real world environment. Ensuring this second order risk assessment is performed not just at project initiation, but continually throughout project execution, is a fundamental leadership responsibility, informed by ongoing PCM Assessment and supported by the Systems Approach to be discussed below. *Continually* is the key word. No ship's captain switches off the radar on leaving port – but many, many times the risk assessment, so assiduously produced at the beginning of a project, is left to gather dust on the shelf as the project proceeds and reaction (as opposed to proaction) becomes the prevailing activity.

Appreciative Judgement is hard to develop, for it tends to be constrained within a reference class that is limited by experience. Typically, we can only 'see' risk within that reference class; and addressing this weakness provides an additional argument for the application of both Experiential Learning and the System Approach as discussed below.

RISK DENIAL

> *They couldn't hit an elephant at this dist...*
> General John Sedgwick, shot by a Confederate
> sharpshooter in the American Civil war

The most prevalent difficulty with second order risk in complex PM is the exponentially greater psychological tendency to denial – a simple refusal to face facts, even in the face of compelling evidence, which may be down to a fear of making a wrong decision but is more likely to be an overriding desire to believe that the situation couldn't really happen, because its consequence is just too awful to contemplate. This is seen often, at human '*not everyone who smokes/drinks/has unprotected sex gets Lung Cancer/liver disease/ AIDS*'; organisational '*The bank is just too big to fail/ we're too good to be relegated*'; and project '*The 'O' ring won't shatter just because it's cold (the cause of the Challenger Space Shuttle disaster) /we'll catch up on the schedule later*' levels. It gets worse – and more difficult to counter – the more complex (and therefore more public) the project, since the accusation of a U-turn or the need to avoid being seen as 'faint-hearted' is a threat to both power and position.

Strong leadership can be dangerous in such situations – particularly if it involves refusing to accept the truth. Lawrence McDonald, the author of the definitive history of the Lehman Brothers downfall, says it takes just one phrase to understand the failure: '*24,992 people striving hard, making money, and about eight guys losing it*' (McDonald 2009).

The need is for leadership that is strong enough to hear the truth, and courageous enough to face it. Winston Churchill: '*I say to the House as I said to ministers who have joined this government, I have nothing to offer but blood, toil, tears, and sweat. We have before us an ordeal of the most grievous kind. We have before us many, many months of struggle and suffering.*'

Risk denial is not quite the same as turning a blind eye, which we could euphemistically term 'intelligent denial'. Nelson knew the Danish ships were there at the battle of Copenhagen – he just decided to take the risk, more confident in his fleet's ability than was the admiral who had told him to disengage. (He didn't actually say '*I see no ships*' – but '*I really do not see the signal*'. Not quite as good a soundbite, though). However 'intelligent' in hindsight, it is just as dangerous. Nelson's 'courageous leadership' is praised because he won the bet. But it *was* a bet. As, in truth, was Churchill's acceptance of the challenge rather than negotiating a peace, as so many advised. But, according to one historian, his defiant speeches in the dark days of 1940 created '*the euphoria of irrational belief in ultimate victory*', and that euphoria carried his people with him. They were lucky – but perhaps luck is just an attribute of leadership. Thomas Jefferson: '*I'm a great believer in luck, and I find the harder I work, the more I have of it.*'

THE CONSPIRACY OF OPTIMISM

In a similar vein, courageous leadership must also recognise and address what has come to be known as the 'Conspiracy of Optimism' (CoO) – although the term 'Conspiracy to gain Approvals' may be more accurate.

> *I want this project. You want this project. If we tell our sponsors how much it would really cost/how long it would really take they wouldn't agree. So lie to me please – I will know you're lying, but I won't challenge you. By the time they find out, you and I will probably have moved on anyway. And you just never know – nothing might go wrong, expected risks will never materialise, we could have got it absolutely right first time – even though none of these have ever been the case before, it might just have been bad luck.*

The central issue is unsurprisingly – about people. Typically, in large projects, the main actors are in mid-career, with important and well-paid jobs, which they hold down on the basis of perceived success – usually measured over very short timeframes. It would be rare for such people not to need the job and the money that goes with it – and therefore they feel they must continually reinforce that perception of success in the minds of both those to whom they report, and across each stakeholder interface. Supplier Project Managers want to give their own management and their customers good news stories; in turn, their sponsors – both shareholders and governments – want to be able to report success, in the face of a media which delights in bad news.

It is unusual for such projects to be cancelled. When things go wrong, a public flogging of one or two scapegoats will normally be deemed sufficient *pour encourager les autres*, but the project will probably plod on regardless, despite its lateness or profligacy resulting in undeclared detrimental effects on overall strategies, not to mention other dependent projects. The potential consequences – in the defence sector to national security; in the commercial sector to survival; in humanitarian projects to life itself – are unacceptable; and the PM community should beware any complacency and an attitude that says it doesn't really matter, let's just convince ourselves that it'll all come right in the end.

The CoO is fuelled by three parties. Project sponsors have a vision (a 'want') which is generally technically uninformed, but which will delight their public; the purchaser community is prepared to skew information in order to get the result they consider the sponsor *ought* to want (the 'need'); and the suppliers are trying to prevail in an increasingly competitive market, made worse by an unhealthy economic climate. The end user – in public sector projects the taxpayer, in the private sector the investor – place their trust in these three parties to deliver for the greater good. Unfortunately, the outlook is getting worse, in terms of both schedule delay and cost overrun. De facto, projects are inevitably becoming more complex (the easy ones have already been done). We cannot afford not to get better.

Clearly, someone has to take responsibility, and it has to start at the top. Bernard Gray, the author of the UK report into defence acquisition:

> *Across the piece, there will be a need for consistent leadership and courage. Ministers will have to be prepared to take on vested interests, often within the ranks of their own civil servants. They will have to stick to their guns when leaking and counter-briefing starts. The interests of public servants who dare to try to innovate within the public service must be promoted. From my experience of working in and with the Ministry of Defence over the past decade I know how strong such vested interests are and how much commitment is required to overcome resistance to change.*
>
> *(Gray 2009)*

In addition to courageous and tenacious leadership, other essential keywords are realism – speaking truth to power; planning – and refusing to proceed until plans have been comprehensively validated; and empathy, the art of being able to see through the eyes of others. Funnily enough, though, these attributes could simply be regarded as fundamental aspects of leadership in any case. Mutual co-operation between all stakeholders, based on the good of the project not parochialism, begins with the understanding that the outcomes can only ever be win–win or lose–lose. Other than in sport, a win–lose result doesn't really happen in the real world.

The issue is further exacerbated within the prevailing market economy, and it has to be asked if a CoO is an inevitable consequence of this. While a competitive acquisition environment undoubtedly has its benefits, it also has negative effects – '*it's not just what competition does for you, it's also about what it does to you.*' In the scramble to reach an agreement, decisions are often made too early, long before the uncertainty that invariably accompanies complex projects can be attenuated, and certainly before other systemic risks – social issues, the emergent effect on other projects and systems and the human elements – have been identified, analysed and understood. Whether this is due to the relative difficulty in measuring these effects, or simply because people don't want to know the answers, is debatable

It is tautological to assert that estimates are only that – estimates. They are based on contemporary understanding, not facts – and may not – *must* not – be considered immalleable in the longer term. Yet once initial project budgets and schedules are set, based on such estimates, they have immense staying power, even to the extent that over time, system functionality and project resources are sacrificed in order to achieve what was unrealistic in the first place. '*Plans are always based on what you won the contract at.*' There is an element of pride in this – it is a sign of weakness to admit that you might have been wrong, and when pride is coupled with an emotional attachment to previous statements, it is very tempting to make decisions that justify the past rather than address the future.

It is interesting to consider the changed behavioural approach to projects that are considered urgent – disaster relief being a prime example. 80 per cent solutions, implemented quickly, are far more use than 100 per cent performance delivered too late. In 'non-urgent' projects, the aspiration to perfection will never be achievable (but engineers will always tend to look for it anyway).

IMPROVISATIONAL MANAGEMENT

> *We all do 'do, re, mi', but you have to find the other notes yourself.*
> *Louis Armstrong*

The British comedian Les Dawson used to have a regular routine in which he would sit at the piano and play a piece including several off-key chords. Funnily enough, this improved his reputation as a musician – people would nod wisely and say, '*It's really difficult to play the wrong notes, you know; it takes a talented pianist to play that badly.*' There are those who would say that some modern jazz players are more in the tradition of Dawson than Delius; the notes they play appear to be random. Yet in truth, musical improvisation is both structured and disciplined, allowing groups of musicians to create coherent work without (apparently) having planned or rehearsed, and soloists to work with a backing ensemble who they may never even have met beforehand.

An interesting comparison can be made between this ability and real-time, under-pressure management decision-making processes. Musical improvisation demands a knowledge of theory (first order methods); an agreed key, time signature and chord progression (the organisational standard process guidelines); and that the player (Project Manager) has a mastery, not only of these things, but the ability *and confidence* to deploy them to create a unique and context-relevant performance which satisfies both him/herself, the audience, and the composer's intention (pan-stakeholder outcome delivery). This confidence stems not just from rehearsal, but the practitioners ability to reflect-in-practice – in other words, to be constantly aware of oneself and ones place in the surroundings — albeit not necessarily consciously. The psychology professor Mihaly Csikszentmihalyi refers to this as 'flow':

> *The state in which people are so involved in an activity that nothing else seems to matter; the experience itself is so enjoyable that people will do it even at great cost, for the sheer sake of doing it ... The ego falls away. Time flies. Every action, movement, and thought follows inevitably from the previous one, like playing jazz. Your whole being is involved, and you're using your skills to the utmost.*
>
> *(Csikszentmihalyi 1990)*

This mental state of total immersion in the task-at-hand is often described by practitioners in many different fields, from sport through music to management, as being 'in the groove' – 'inside the music' – 'in the zone' – 'on top of the game' – totally energised and focussed. It describes the second order leader perfectly.

Second order leadership has a vision, and communicates that vision clearly across the whole stakeholder community, both internally and externally; it doesn't deny uncertainty and risk, but neither does it rely on luck to see things through; and especially, it is unprepared to sacrifice long-term success in favour of perceived short-term reward.

Ultimately it seeks to deliver against a fit-for-purpose, mutually agreed, product/ service *outcome* – and is unafraid to change approach and tactics when an existing course would fail to deliver it. In fact, it finds no alternative but to do so. Martin Luther: '*Here I stand. I can do no other. God help me. Amen.*'

And it *loves* what it does.

CHAPTER 4

OUTCOMES AND ETHICS

MANAGING FOR OUTCOME

> *A means can be justified only by its end. But the end in its turn needs to be justified.*
>
> Leon Trotsky

> *In the beginning of the malady it is easy to cure but difficult to detect, but in the course of time, not having been either detected or treated, it becomes easy to detect but difficult to cure.*
>
> Niccolo Machiavelli

March 2, 1969. I can clearly remember watching the first Concorde flight. There had never been such a breathtakingly beautiful aircraft! It looked as though it didn't need engines at all – just a slight push at the end of the runway and it would soar into the sky like a paper dart. What a contrast to the great lumbering jumbo jets! I had seen the future of air travel, and it was a triumph of Anglo–French design and engineering excellence.

Except it wasn't. Heavy fuel consumption, small fuel tanks, noise and exhaust pollution (and possibly some transatlantic political jealousy) rendered it a white elephant which, apart from its use as a prestige luxury transport towards the end of its life, was economically unviable. The designers produced an aircraft to a specification. One suspects that no one told them to accommodate the likely impact of external events, in particular the possibility of an oil crisis coupled with a growing awareness of environmental issues, and the risk inherent in the assumption that the main route would be transatlantic. Possibly, they could have addressed these issues in the design, at least in part – but if not, the unfeasibility of the project would have been apparent from the beginning.

Actually, what makes it worse is that this unfeasibility *was* predicted – and received wisdom has it that if it were not for a no-cancellation clause in the original joint contract, imposed because of a deep-seated lack of mutual trust between the two governments, Concorde would never have gone into production at all. We may have missed seeing a thing of beauty – but beauty is more than skin deep.

The history of major projects is littered all around with similar stories; ships that have been obsolete even before their maiden voyage, new towns that no one wants to live in, bridges to nowhere. The difficulties in cancelling such projects when they are in progress are often insuperable; with hindsight, it is often clear that they should never have been started in the first place, and that this was known. Human nature is enthusiastically optimistic, though – we long to get started, and we want no Cassandra to warn us of the consequence – quite the contrary – when proposed projects *have* been cancelled after a feasibility study proved them unviable, the instigators of those studies have been vilified for wasting money and lacking the courage or the management skill to proceed.

It has long been known that the cheapest point to fix in-service errors is at the design phase, where the majority of them have their origin, as Figure 4.1 shows.

The biggest in-service error of all, of course, is to build entirely the wrong thing. First order techniques will deliver against a firm, documented, functional requirement. But it's mostly the non-functional (usually unspecified) requirements that bite, the most significant of these being fitness for purpose in the target operational environment and the interaction with other, uncontrollable components within it. But this is not the only outcome to consider.

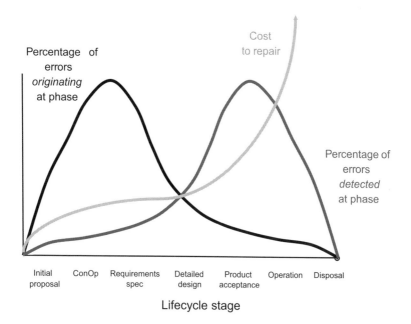

Figure 4.1   In-service errors
Source: Adapted from Barry Boehm, *Software Engineering Economics* (1981).

The typical project feasibility study considers the likely organisational rewards against the organisational cost. What it often fails to do is consider the wider scope, the consequence that project implementation will have on external, apparently unrelated, systems. Neither does it consider that desirable outcomes change over time, and that immediate benefit has to be weighed against a final outcome which may only be realised some considerable time later.

Requirements Management is concerned with what a product or service should do, and how it performs against the documented specification; whereas the purpose of Outcome Management is to deliver the effect. There are many excellent first order tools to address the former; but Outcome Management is very definitely a second order issue. Put another way, First Order PM delivers the change, but not necessarily the desired result. The two things are not the same; neither is 'want' necessarily the same as 'need'.

What people 'want' is limited by their prejudice and knowledge of what is available and possible – encapsulated in the German word 'Weltanschauung', which roughly translates as 'Worldview' but really means more than that – it is the (often unexamined and/or non-explicit) outlook or assumption which makes a change desirable – '*The way the world looks from where I'm standing at this precise moment, viewed through my past experience, prejudice, hopes and dreams – and conditioned by the burdens I currently carry.*'

Unfortunately, since each person's Weltanschauung is unique to them, their view of what is wanted (let alone what is needed) will also differ, sometimes profoundly – a four-year-old's idea of an ideal mid-morning snack may be a bar of chocolate-covered toffee as opposed to the raw carrot proposed by its mother. Given that, by definition, complex projects will have many stakeholders, this is potentially a major problem, at its worst when the end user of the product or service is not involved in the specification. A recent example is soldiers using their own personal mobile phones in preference to the hugely expensive battlefield radio systems provided through the official procurement channels, which are not only too heavy and cumbersome, but complex to use and lacking in equivalent capacity. Involving the users (in the case the soldiers themselves) in the requirement stage might have been a good idea...

Production of a Concept of Operation, or 'ConOps' addresses this issue. There are a number of techniques for the development and production of a ConOps – Use Cases, Scenario Planning, Business Process Modelling, the Soft Systems Methodology (SSM) and several others, most of which have commercial tool support. The System Anatomy process, described later and more fully in the Appendix, is an attempt to synthesise these into a process that is simple and straightforward enough to be used at the very highest conceptual level; its output then forming the foundation for more detailed, lower-level analysis and conceptual planning. A ConOps should allow all *(ALL!)*

stakeholders to document their own, subjective, description of what they would consider to be a success – what good looks like for them, in other words. The fact that some of these may be invalid or unachievable is irrelevant – in fact it is invaluable, in that it is by far better to discover unrealistic views at the earliest possible stage, in order to manage expectations. Unless an accommodation is reached between these, it is almost impossible for the delivered product to be universally considered successful.

Experience with past projects makes it imperative to ensure that stakeholder inputs are given equal weight. Too often, a small supplier's opinion has been disregarded by a much larger customer, only for the importance of their specific knowledge to be recognised much later on when the product is found to be at best suboptimal, at worst completely unfit for purpose.

ConOps must address through-life issues – what is needed now may not be the same as the need over time; this is especially important when the product development cycle is likely to be of long duration. A well-known example is the deployment of military equipment designed to meet a once-perceived threat from the Soviet bloc, but which is of little use in the asymmetric warfare of today. It is essential to perform continuous analysis of the external environment; the original PEST (Political, Economic, Social, and Technological) approach has been extended by experience with a number of variations – my own preference being STEEPLED (Social, Technical, Economic, Environmental, Political, Legal, Educational and Demographic).

It is also necessary to consider other, possibly ostensibly unrelated, systems that the product/service may affect or be affected by. The problem of emergence is very real – and almost inevitable in complex systems. Individual products which work perfectly well in isolation exhibit totally different characteristics when used together – the whole becomes greater than the sum of its parts. This may be a good thing – but it may not. The battlefield radio mentioned above initially used frequencies that were the same as the equipment used to detect

Improvised Explosive Devices (IEDs), meaning that soldiers couldn't use their radio at the same time as their IED detector.

It is the result that matters. Unless 'outcome' is the project driver, constantly revalidated against the current business situation and future strategy, the project will always be at risk. Even if delivered to time, cost and quality, the wrong thing will always be the wrong thing. The ConOps, mutually agreed across all stakeholders, is the only sure way of informing agreement of the *right* thing; and the only way of guaranteeing the validity of the ConOps is to adopt a Systems Approach to deliverable production, not to mention its suitability not just for the organisation, its customers, but also the outside world. Indeed, it may in the future become mandatory for complex projects to be able to prove that they have used best efforts to analyse outcomes; for there is a wider dimension to all this.

OUTCOMES AND ETHICS

> *The release of atom power has changed everything except our way of thinking. If I had known to what my research would lead, I would have become a watchmaker.*
>
> Albert Einstein

Consider the following scenario. You are a conscientious, morally responsible research scientist, working for a global organisation that rewards you well and provides strong support for your work without interfering. You discover a method to provide clean, ridiculously cheap energy that more than satisfies the whole world's needs, and will not only bring huge profits to your company, but will also relieve world poverty and hunger virtually at a stroke. There is a problem, however, that *only you* are aware of. Once the power is switched on, it cannot ever be turned off – and there is a 99 per cent chance that in 150 years' time, it will explode and blow the Earth apart. What do you do?

Your decision is a classic ethical dilemma. The choice is between doing what you are paid to do and publishing your findings, or burning your research notes because the consequence of publication is unthinkable. We term the former an ethic of duty, the latter an ethic of consequence.

Duty ethics run the risk of people performing unspeakable acts (*'I was only following orders'*). Consequence ethics are only as good as your powers of prediction. How do you know it's 99 per cent? Are you positive it's not 98 per cent? Or 90 per cent? Or 9 per cent? And how can you be so sure that we won't discover a way to stop it within the next 150 years, anyway?

This is not a science fiction scenario – unforeseen (possibly!) consequences of technological progress have happened throughout history. Tobacco was seen as a wonder drug, curing all known maladies (and if you don't believe me, read Spenser's *Faerie Queene*). Chlorofluorocarbons (CFCs) were a singularly Good Thing; their inertness made sure that the pollution risk was minimised. Nuclear fission has a million and one uses for the benefit of humanity, and only two to its detriment. Applied to bring pain relief to those in agony, diamorphine is a great blessing; we call it smack, though, when used for other purposes. Most recently, on the very day that BP was to receive an award for 'outstanding safety and pollution prevention performance in offshore operations', it's 'failsafe' systems failed. Clearly, they didn't do what it said on the packet.

Ethical consideration and consideration of the wider consequences of product implementation as part of the PM process was for a long time regarded at best as a sideline issue, sometimes worse, in a business environment where a duty ethic prevailed. Milton Friedman, at the beginning of the decade of greed, was unequivocal. *'Few trends could so thoroughly undermine the very foundations of our free society as the acceptance by corporate officials of a social responsibility other than to make as much money for their stockholders as possible. This is a fundamentally subversive doctrine'* (Friedman 1970).

Only a few years later, it is unusual to find a major organisation that does not consider ethical governance and consequence analysis as a major component of the senior management portfolio. The change was not due to a Damascene conversion in the boardroom; it was a much more pragmatic driver than that. Immanuel Kant offered the rule, '*Act only upon that maxim which you can at the same time will that it should become a universal law.*' Writing today, he may have modified this for today's litigious society to read: '*Act only on that maxim which you can defend in a court of law.*'

Outcome Management is not just about realising the project's business objectives – it must encompass the effects of product implementation on a much wider scale, and again, I suggest that the only way that such effects can be identified and addressed is the adoption of a Systems methodology.

SECOND ORDER TOOLS AND TACTICS

CHAPTER 5

THE SYSTEMS APPROACH TO PROJECT MANAGEMENT

To be able to see the world globally, which you are going to have to be able to do, and to see it as a world of unique individuals ... that is really complexity.

C. West Churchman

No man is an island,
Entire of itself.
Each is a piece of the continent,
A part of the main.
If a clod be washed away by the sea,
Europe is the less.
As well as if a promontory were.
As well as if a manner of thine own
Or of thine friend's were.
Each man's death diminishes me,
For I am involved in mankind.
Therefore, send not to know
For whom the bell tolls,
It tolls for thee.

John Donne

SYSTEMS THINKING, CYBERNETICS AND MODELLING

If I were asked to recommend the one single essential book for Project Managers, it would be Ian Mitroff and Harold Linstone's *The Unbounded Mind* (1993) It profoundly changed my professional thinking, opened new avenues of enquiry, inspired me in many different ways; and I readily acknowledge my debt to it.

To see the world as an interconnected whole, as they suggest, is to understand that every person, however unique, has some form of relationship; and that these relationships are constantly changing as the people themselves change.

The same applies to systems – however isolated they appear, they influence each other, albeit to a lesser or degree. The world is a mess – the term coined by Russell Ackoff as representing '*situations comprising complex systems of strongly interacting problems*' – and reflecting on the phenomenon of emergence discussed earlier, he asserts that, '*The behaviour of a mess depends more on how its parts interact than on how they act independently of each other*' (Ackoff 1999).

What is important to a Project Manager is to identify those interactions that are significant – and there will be more than you think. Classical analysis methods attempt to understand how things work by decomposing them; but clearly, breaking them down into their component parts cannot address emergent problems. Systems Thinking works the other way round, identifying the interactions between components to discover what happens when they are combined. It attempts to predict the violence of the Texas tornado caused by a butterfly flapping its wings in Brazil. Perhaps the best-known approaches are Peter Checkland's SSM (1981) and the Peter Senge's *Fifth Discipline* (1990), but there are several others.

The common element of all these is that they seek first to identify the purpose of the system to be developed – to answer the question: 'What is this Bridge/Boat/Olympic Games/ Organisation a system to do?' at the highest possible level. Possibly the best example of this was an incoming chief executive of a commercial TV station asking the question of his entire workforce. The answers he got varied according to the various roles performed in different departments – '*to entertain, to inform, to produce programmes, to sell advertising*'. No, he said. '*All of these are activities we must do well, but they are not the overall unifying purpose. **We are a system to create tailored audiences for our advertisers.** Everything we do is a subsystem of that overall system.*

Once the highest-level purpose is established, it is then possible to consider the ways in which that purpose is achieved, and everything we do must contribute to its achievement.'

Systems Thinking is a method of enquiry into a situation in which a problem exists or transformation is needed, to identify the internal and external interactions, and to consider possible solutions – that is, what needs to be produced, what is 'the right thing'; it does not necessarily provide an answer as to *how* to produce it. It has to be accompanied by an approach which seeks to identify the organisation and plan that would best enact the required change, and this is where Cybernetics makes its contribution. Cybernetics – a word derived from the Greek meaning 'steersman', or 'pilot' – is usually defined as the study of control and communication in the animal and the machine, or sometimes as the science of effective organisation; and the most important concept in Cybernetic theory is that of requisite variety.

Variety is the number of possible states of a system. Ross Ashby's law of requisite variety states that, *'Only Variety can absorb variety – the variety in the control system must be equal to or larger than the variety of the perturbations in order to achieve control.* A simpler way of putting it might be that to control anything at all, you need more answers than there are possible questions. A topical example might be the so-called 'war on the drug smuggling cartels', where a police force operating under the rule of law will possess insufficient variety to control, by force alone, an enemy which is totally unconstrained and can use whatever degree of violence it wishes. Requisite variety can be obtained in two ways. A variety attenuator reduces the number of possible states of the system; a variety amplifier increases the number of control mechanisms. In the above example, variety in the system might be attenuated by restricting the number of routes along which drugs can be transported and increasing the number of searches on the remaining open routes; control variety could be amplified by increasing the penalty for trafficking to a level where people are not prepared to take the risk.

The organisation must therefore be designed with sufficient variety to address whatever events or changes may occur in the system under development. These mechanisms will include the ability to identify such issues as early as possible, to assess them and to put in place actions to cater for them, and this demands a structure which is flexible enough to deal with whatever storms may come. Flexibility wins. Every time.

The Viable System Model (VSM) proposed by Stafford Beer (Beer 1985) likens the organisation to the human body, with eyes and ears that can tell the brain what is happening, enabling it to make decisions; and a nervous system that can communicate to the skeleton-muscular system what to do about it. In practice, we have found the VSM is extremely useful in ensuring an appropriate high-level programme or project organisational design, but our experience has also shown that a lower-level, detailed approach can be more useful at lower, subsystem levels.

This is achieved by the application of Business Process Modelling methods to represent the actual processes that support the design, validation and delivery of a solution that achieves the system purpose. Although many modelling tools, such as the IDEF (Integration DEFintion) family, Unified Modelling Language (UML) and others, have tended to be developed within the software-intensive project area, they are applicable on a much wider basis. The incorporation of simulation and graphical representation is especially useful.

When System Thinking methods are placed alongside Cybernetics and Business Process Modelling, the three approaches combine to provide a hugely powerful second order toolset, providing the foundation on which first order tools can then build in order to deliver the right thing the right way in a complex project environment.

Unfortunately, experience has shown the greatest difficulty with this approach in project organisations is the attitude of many people (especially very senior managers) which leads them to distrust what they perceive as 'philosophical' or 'academic' methods, and who, in the absence of a structured approach to outcome definition, often make decisions on a subjective basis without necessarily accommodating wider stakeholder viewpoints.

To address this, along with client colleagues, we developed an approach termed a Systems Anatomy which, while based on recognised methods such as SSM, the VSM, IDEF and others, is simplified to make it amenable to regular iteration and modification in response to changes in the external environment and to be 'accessible' to relevant stakeholders at all levels despite their scepticism.

THE SYSTEMS ANATOMY

There are tens, if not hundreds, of strategic project planning, outcome definition, organisational design and requirements capture methods. In practice, some work; most don't. Not because they are inherently wrong, but because they are either so complex or exhaustive that once the process is complete, there is an inevitable reluctance to start again. Unfortunately, the wider environment – 'everything that isn't me', as Einstein defined it – never stands still, and the grandest plans and structures become increasingly irrelevant every single day. What is needed is a high-level method that is simple, straightforward and amenable to continuous environmental change; and which can form the basis on which more formalised, in-depth studies can be subsequently performed if required. It is critically important that it be flexible and easy to both understand and use if it is to be able to respond very quickly to the changing issues of a highly dynamic environment.

An example, used in our own consultancy practice, is termed System Anatomy Modelling. This is a process that can be used on its own or in conjunction with other classical methods, enabling rapid, continuous assessment of the relevance of outcomes, strategies and structures. While based on formal systems methodologies, it emphasises simplicity and usability. After initial incremental development and application, it has subsequently been deployed in many organisations, ranging from the production of an operational strategy for a small service company up to the successful comprehensive organisational transformation of a multi-billion pound engineering programme. In every case, the results offered new – and often surprising – insight into business operations and the organisational design appropriate to supporting them. The case study in Appendix 1 describes the process in practice.

Useful as it has proved, however, Systems Anatomy Modelling is by no means the only way of applying a Systems Thinking approach combined with Cybernetic and modelling techniques; if the organisational culture allows, it may be that other, rather more rigorous, methods are appropriate. All I would suggest is that it is the minimum acceptable level of the application of Systems Thinking to outcome definition and cross-stakeholder agreement in early lifecycle analysis.

Following its development, as described in the case study, System Anatomy Modelling has been applied many times in widely differing situations and projects. But it is important to say that this has not happened as an automatic consequence of applying the process – it is not a standalone panacea. Many proprietary slimming products carry small print which says something like, 'Works best as part of a calorie-controlled diet', and there are parallels here. Whatever level of process is adopted, it is important to remember they are only part of the Second Order PM toolset; their effectiveness is constrained by the accuracy, breadth and depth of the input to them, and this brings us to consider how this may be enhanced.

CHAPTER 6

EXPERIENTIAL LEARNING

Only everyone can know the truth.

Wolfgang von Goethe

*We learn from experience that men never
learn anything from experience.*

George Bernard Shaw

REPERTOIRE

The key element of successful decision making is the 'repertoire' of
the decision maker. Repertoire is a combination of three aspects – an
ability to 'see' or (better) 'appreciate', an ability to 'do', and an ability
to 'judge', it applies at both personal and organisational levels.

A professional racing driver approaching a bend at 200 mph 'sees'
much more of the situation than would a learner even at one tenth of
that speed – traffic, the state of the track, tyre wear, the championship
table, the personality, skill and likely behaviour of the other drivers,
the responsiveness of his own car – and 'seeing' these factors, thus
has a much broader set of possible actions from which to select
when searching for the most appropriate response to them, using his
judgement to determine which action will result in the best outcome.

In exactly the same way, a good leader will wish to gain the broadest
possible appreciation of a problem situation and then assess the capability
at his or her disposal, before assessing the feasibility and relative merits
of different possible responses and selecting the most effective.

The Systems approaches discussed above can help with all these aspects, particularly with respect to modelling different courses of action and designing the response; but it will inevitably be constrained by a) the breadth of the initial appreciation, which will be restricted to the already 'known knowns' and 'known unknowns', and b) the existing capability – what we are actually able to do about it, and this latter will vary from person to person, organisation to organisation. It's no good my simply 'appreciating' the 200mph bend with Michael Schumacher's eyes; if I can't control the car with his level of skill, there are some actions which, although perfectly possible for him, would be suicidal for me. Repertoire development cannot just be restricted to extending appreciative ability – it has to address action as well.

What is needed are ways of both reducing the 'unknown unknowns', and at the same time increasing our capability. In the terms introduced earlier, this attenuates the variety in the system and amplifies the control variety. We call this 'learning', and learning is a combination of both training and education. These are not the same thing, and they achieve different results. To determine which is relevant, we need to understand the so-called 'cognitive hierarchy', shown in Figure 6.1.

At the lowest level, data is simply a record of a historical event, in some form of language – either letters or numbers. It doesn't actually mean anything. Data has to be assembled into some recognised order if it is to become in any way meaningful – and in so doing becomes Information, which we could think of as words. But Information itself is also abstract until placed alongside some real-world issue-at-hand, when it becomes what we normally term Knowledge – just as words only achieve meaning when put into a sentence. At one level, knowledge can be articulated and documented as a set of rules or facts which can be systematically applied – the term 'explicit' knowledge is commonly used to describe this. 'Tacit' knowledge, one the other hand, cannot be written down. It develops over time, with reflection, practice and experience. As an example, even though it comes with an instruction manual, and despite what it says on the box, it isn't possible to build a flat pack bookshelf without a certain level of

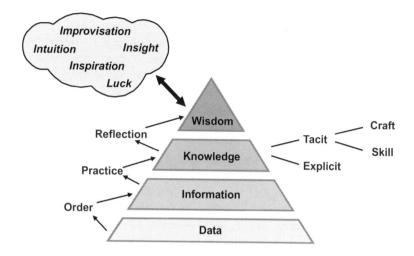

Figure 6.1   Cognitive hierarchy

skill in joinery. Skill, refined by many years of continuous learning, may evolve into craftsmanship – it takes a cabinet maker, not an amateur joiner, to build a Chippendale armchair. At a higher level still, Wisdom is the ability not just to know *how* to do something, but to appreciate *what* is needed; Aristotle refers to it as the ability to 'see through' things – what we referred to earlier as 'appreciation'. Sometimes, it may even be referred to by other names: intuition, imagination, insight, instinct, inspiration, improvisational ability, even luck! (Which is not necessarily the same as magic; Napoleon chose his generals on the basis of luck rather than breeding; the golfer Gary Player (borrowing from Thomas Jefferson) once said '*s 'funny – the more I practice, the luckier I get*'; in our own experience, lucky leaders tend to be those who pay attention to honesty and fairness in relationships at all levels).

If the complex project environment were stable, and if actions and decisions could be defined as processes, people could be trained (perhaps 'programmed' would be a better word) to respond. But it isn't.

Training gives people the specific knowledge of 'how' to do things. The training process articulates and documents the source information through books, courses, video and suchlike, and is capable of doing this even at a distance. But the learning is not complete; until the theory has been put into practice, we cannot say we know how to do something. You can't learn to ride a bike just by reading about it.

Wisdom, though, is even more than this; it is the ability to create new 'knowledge' as an emergent property of the combination of several mutually unrelated knowledges, and offers the ability to understand 'what' to do and 'why' it should be done. Training produces capability; but developing wisdom demands education. Wisdom is unarticulatable – it develops through reflection on experience, as will be explained below – and this, too, needs to be practiced, in both senses of the word. Aristotle: '*We are what we repeatedly do. Excellence, then, is not an act, but a habit.*'

Training and Education can be termed as *adaptive* and *generative* forms of learning. Adaptive learning is appropriate when the problem is clearly articulated and understood, and the environment in which it lies is bounded. If the problem situation is known, it can be analysed and articulated; a rigorously structured training programme will enable people to recognise situations within a previously defined classification, then respond according to an equally previously defined process. Generative learning, however, is the way wisdom is developed; it has been described as '*the active process of saying "Oh, that's like ..." the process of constructing links between new and old knowledge, or a personal understanding of how new ideas fit into an individual's web of known concepts.*' This is the essence of wisdom – the ability to combine unrelated knowledges in order to 'see through' an issue-at-hand which has never been previously encountered or even anticipated. Generative learning can never be 'trained' – it develops through an educational process which allows people the freedom, and gives them the capacity, to perform this construction without constraint. Education, therefore, needs to be as broad as possible. Sir Geoffrey Vickers: '*Even the dogs may eat of the crumbs that fall from*

the rich man's table; and in these days, when the rich in knowledge eat
such specialised food at such separate tables, only the dogs have the
chance of a balanced diet' (Vickers 1965).

THE LEARNING CYCLE

The generative learning process is essentially experiential, drawing
its lessons from three sources – from oneself, from others in the
organisation, and from other organisations. In all three cases,
the learning comes not simply from having the experience, but
understanding what really happened and the reasons behind these
outcomes; extracting the fundamental lessons from these which can
be extrapolated into other similar situations; testing the validity of
this extrapolation – and then applying these lessons in practice by
modifying existing behaviour. The best approach to describe the
process by which this understanding can be gained – the way in which
sense is made of events, and capability enhanced – is to consider the
'Learning Cycle'.

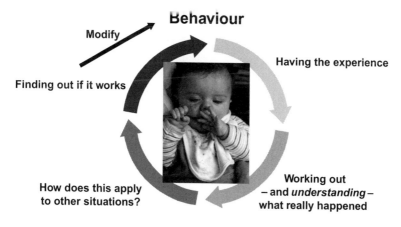

Figure 6.2   The Learning Cycle

The illustration of my grandson Daniel practicing generative learning on a bowl of spaghetti bolognese in Figure 6.2 illustrates this learning cycle. Babies are extremely adept learners. Children are good. Secondary school pupils are OK. Undergraduates retain some ability. But when people start work, organisational culture tends to beat any generative learning capability out of them. An attitude of, *'You're not paid to think, you're paid to work! Think in your own time!'* combined with a *'Just do it'* philosophy will soon eliminate any subversive inclination to reflect before action. Having said which, the one-time president of EDS, H. Ross Perot, when accused of precipitate action, agreed that, *'Our approach has sometimes been "Ready, fire, aim"... but at least it's better than General Motors "Ready, aim, aim, aim, aim ..."'* Perhaps Napoleon got the balance right – *'Take time to deliberate, but when the time for action has arrived, stop thinking and go in.'*

Experiential Learning is not a luxury, but an absolute necessity in any second order management toolset. This demands that the Learning Cycle should be institutionalised in every organisation that seeks to execute complex projects. Experience must first be captured; analysed; its lessons abstracted; recorded in a taxonomised form that is straightforward and accessible; disseminated; and finally applied. Many organisations would already claim to do this – they proudly talk about their 'lessons learned process'. They deceive themselves. Unless all the activities of the Learning Cycle are performed, at best all they are doing is data collection. This meaningless data is then typically placed into what a rather disillusioned Project Manager once termed a 'write-only' database, since without a standard taxonomy it is incapable of being retrieved and the 'lessons' impossible to disseminate or apply. Such organisations make the same mistakes over and over again, and never think to ask why.

PROJECT LEARNING

There are three different types of learning activity which take place both within each phase and over the complete life of a project – irrespective of its size. As the project proceeds, so the learning emphasis moves from Enquiry, through Capture, into Reflection and Analysis – although these stages will inevitably overlap – see Figure 6.3. The cycle will be reiterated within each lifecycle phase – in effect, each phase being considered a project in its own right.

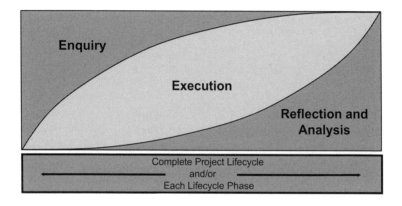

Figure 6.3   Learning in the lifecycle

Learning in the lifecycle

At the early (and most critical) stages of strategy formulation, negotiation, phase initiation, requirements capture/specification/ validation and high-level design, the emphasis is on Enquiry, and learning provision needs to direct and facilitate the capture of wisdom gained from both internal and external sources of previous experience. Examples of techniques applicable at this stage might be searches on a Learning Library of similar past projects, the use of Scenario Planning workshops, and straightforward desk research. The generic process is shown below in Figure 6.4.

Figure 6.4   Learning at the Enquiry stage

Learning at the Enquiry stage

The emphasis changes as the project moves into the detailed design, integration and production phases – the Execution stage (Figure 6.5). Here it becomes increasingly important to be aware of what is actually happening, of what progress is *really* being made, and of any scope or schedule changes and external events which may need a response. Truthful (the truth, the whole truth, and nothing but the truth!) project diaries should be maintained, not just as a means of project communication, but as a source of future learning; Scenario Planning may be ongoing; in particular, the leadership should be in a constant state of reflection-in-action – where are we? What are we doing? Is it still the right thing to do? Are there better options? What possible external changes could affect us?

Learning during Project Execution

On project completion, after installation and commissioning, comes operation in the target environment, at which point errors made in earlier stages become apparent.

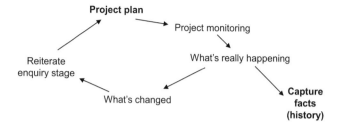

Figure 6.5   Learning during Project Execution

This stage is when Reflection and Analysis (Figure 6.6) allows an understanding of the significance of what was done, and generalised lessons to be captured and recorded in a structured, retrievable form (the Learning Library) for subsequent dissemination. It is important to remember that unless the project stakeholders reflect on the complete project history with total (non-accusatory) honesty and openness, the lessons learned from these latter phases will never be understood, articulated, captured or appropriate process changes made. And with depressing inevitability the same mistakes will be repeated.

REFLECTION AND ANALYSIS

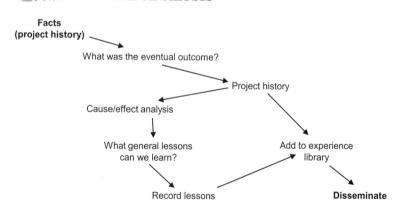

Figure 6.6   Reflection and Analysis

It is quite common to hear people talk about Learning from Experience, and this is certainly necessary at the early and late stages of a project – but by definition, Learning from Experience is post-event. Learning *in* Experience – that is, during Project Execution – is arguably more important, allowing the project team to take account of external factors as they change. No aircraft navigator plots a course before takeoff and then sits back to read the novel they bought at the airport. 'In-flight' course adjustment is a continuous and necessary activity if landfall is to be anywhere near the desired destination. Learning in Experience demands time and space – reflection is hard to do under day-to-day pressure, and it is often the first thing sacrificed to a demanding schedule. This is where strong leadership is needed, insisting on the project team stepping back and thinking about what they are doing, even if the wolves are snapping at their heels; time spent thinking is rarely wasted, it pays back in the number of errors avoided. I remember vividly the CEO of a very large organisation, on hearing of the need for yet another costly remedial task, literally turning purple and banging his fist on the table, screaming, '*Why do we never have the time to get things right the first time, but always have to find the time to put things right afterwards over and over again??!!!*'

EXPERIENTIAL LEARNING TECHNIQUES

As mentioned earlier, different Experiential Learning tools and techniques are appropriate at three main lifecycle phases: at planning and initiation stages, we need to identify and apply relevant past lessons; during project execution, it is necessary to monitor and capture what is happening for reflection and analysis both in experience in order that corrective action may be applied, and from experience, in order to inform future activity. Mark Twain: '*History never repeats itself exactly; but it often rhymes.*'

Post-project (actually, at the end of each project phase, since a project does not end at the point of operational handover, but at disposal) we need to document the lessons learned in a retrievable form. This must be done comprehensively and factually – even though past mistakes may be uncomfortably revealed, the temptation to edit or sanitise has to be avoided if the lessons are really to be learned. One organisation with whom I have worked has an annual Project Management Conference, at which people are encouraged to present case histories of failures. Instead of blame, the atmosphere is one of congratulation and senior management support. If only such leadership maturity were universal. The true cause for shame is making the same mistake twice.

Having said this, it must also be said that 'facts' on their own do not necessarily convey meaning or enable learning. They have to be contextualised, and easily the best way of doing this is by the vehicle of story; and through the ages, story has been used as the basis of wisdom transfer. Stories have the ability to convey deep truths across generational, cultural and even linguistic boundaries in a way that bullet-pointed presentations never will. In our research leading to the development of a portfolio of tools and techniques to facilitate learning as described below, it became very clear that the use of 'story' offered the added benefit that people actually enjoy hearing stories – and when learning is not seen as a chore but as a pleasant experience, it is also at its most effective. We also found that another significant factor in applying the learning tools effectively is a function of senior leadership commitment to their deployment, taking them seriously and participating whenever possible, as opposed to paying lip service by just ticking a 'lessons learned' box and filing them under 'oblivion'.

THE ORGANISATIONAL LIBRARY

All of the techniques that follow will have a 'real-time' benefit, the participants of each event gaining immediate insight into the topics discussed; but their effectiveness will be greatly increased if the lessons are recorded, as documents, reports, case histories, anecdote/story, videos or whatever medium best supports the message.

When I was growing up, my local library in Wythenshawe was hugely important to me, and I cannot pass the building, now closed, without a feeling of gratitude and sadness at its passing. Although there are far fewer public libraries now, and those that do survive are lined with Internet access tables rather than bookshelves, I believe they are of immeasurable value to their local society, not just as places of reference, but of mind-expanding opportunity and centres of community. The Organisational Library has exactly the same function. Certainly it is a repository of lessons and a source of learning; but it has a greater potential than that – it should be a centre for conversation and discussion, a place where ideas may be tested and theories challenged, the hub of wisdom sharing. Every civilisation has had such an entity; Plato had his academy; Native Americans the Chautauqua; the Japanese Dojo, the Indian Ashram, the library at Alexandria, the western University, all fill this role. An excellent modern day example is NASA's Academy of Program/Project & Engineering Leadership (APPEL). Their website is exemplary, and in my view is a credit to both its sponsors and its staff (http://www.nasa.gov/offices/oce/appel/home/index.html). The principle is relevant whatever the organisational size and geographical distribution – the availability of technology making it easier to establish an accessible library than it has ever been, to the extent that the absence of such a facility at organisational level could be argued to be corporate negligence.

Similarity search

A generative learning approach will of necessity be constrained by an individual's past experiences. These restrict her/his vision to within the boundaries they impose, and become that individuals single 'reference class'. In practice, this means that an engineer who has spent 20 years designing bridges, and who is then tasked with delivering an office building, will inevitably adopt bridge design processes and approaches – because these have become the only reference class to which he or she has access. Furthermore, this single reference class imposes the further restriction that every new bridge will be the sum of those before – and any insights from other engineering disciplines will not be taken into consideration.

To counter this restriction, a multi-perspective Similarity Search technique can help enormously. The earlier it is applied in the lifecycle of a new project the better, asking two simple questions: 'What is this project like?' and 'In what ways is it totally unique?' from a wide range of different viewpoints.

For instance, a bridge is like a building because it uses the same process of construction; but a bridge might also be like a motor car because the design process takes much the same level of resource. A bridge might be unlike any other previous bridge because of the volume, or different type, of traffic it has to bear, or the prevailing local geology or weather. As an example of the different similarity types, in our workshops, we ask which of the following is similar to Singapore: is it Norway? The Isle of Wight? The USA? Or Rio de Janeiro? The answer is all of them. Singapore is similar to Norway, because it has the same population; it has the same surface area as the Isle of Wight, and the same per capita GDP as the USA. And it is the same distance from Heathrow as is Rio. All of these similarities might be useful learning opportunities in different ways, according to the task at hand.

Once these similarities and differences have been established, subsequent enquiry is then instigated to look at two further questions:

1. 'What do we know about these?'
2. 'What have we/could we/should we learn from them?'

A more in-depth approach to this is based upon the work done by Niraj Verma (1998), but expanded by experience in our practice into an activity termed a 'Similarity Search'. This groups similarities into basic classifications, asking what other systems share the following characteristics? What questions do these other experiences prompt us to ask?:

Structure – using a bridge example, cantilever, suspension or what? Steel or concrete? Span? Height above the river? Geology of the area? Prevailing weather conditions?
Function – weight, volume and type of traffic? Urban or rural?
Purpose – not just to carry traffic (this is more a function) but is

its purpose Social, for example, joining two communities – Economic? Political? To show the world that we are world class bridge builders? To establish us in the bridge building market?

Values/constraints – deadlines, minimum acceptable Return on Investment to be achieved, is it to be an engineering-led or commercial-led project? Are we building something to last a thousand years? Are we budget-constrained or schedule-constrained?

Relationships – to the system of which it is a component, and to other components of that system – for example, is this bridge to be part of an new integrated transport system? Is there a new massive housing estate/retail park to be built that we don't know about? Or did we think there was to be one which has been cancelled without us knowing? Are we working with customers and suppliers with whom we have never been involved in the past, or are we dealing with the devils we know?

A Similarity Search is not restricted to enquiry on the organisation's own Learning Library, although it will obviously start with the question, 'What else have we done that is similar to what we are about to do?' It is also intended to stretch the boundaries of this enquiry beyond the obvious. As well as including all the project stakeholders in a Similarity Search exercise, building up relationships with other organisations in non-competitive areas can offer significant insight and wisdom sharing opportunity. I once organised a conversation between a group of senior Project Managers in the transport sector and their peers in a defence company. One of the most interesting aspects was their surprise at how many PM issues they had in common, by far the most difficult being people.

Stories by the fireside

Everyone who has run, or attended, a management course will have heard a comment from delegates which roughly goes like this – *'Actually, I felt I learned more in the pub in the evening than I did during the day's lectures.'* In essence, the 'stories by the fireside' approach is about setting a scene in which stories can be told, and consequences, relevancies, lessons and extrapolations explored. It is as far removed from task-oriented, high-pressure course syndicate exercises as it is possible to be, and is the total antithesis of the 'power breakfast'. A guest, who should be someone who commands wide peer respect, or is recognised as having been particularly successful, is invited to share her/his experience in a totally informal setting, with a small group of delegates. The invitation to be a 'guest' should be seen (and promoted) as recognition of a major career contribution. After an informal welcome, and perhaps a buffet, the group retires to a casually laid-out room with some comfortable chairs, and a bottomless pot of coffee. A real fireside makes the setting perfect.

Under the guidance of a facilitator, the guest is introduced – but it is not necessary, in fact not really a good idea at all, to get the group to introduce themselves – this would tend to introduce hierarchy and pecking order which would actually hinder the openness on which this type of event depends.

Facilitators should come equipped with a list of prepared questions, but be prepared to allow the discussion to take its own course. A set of sample questions might be as follows:

- Tell us briefly how you got to be sitting there … the story so far …
- If you were asked to pass on the three most valuable things you've learned in your entire career, what would they be? How did you learn them?
- Who did *you* learn from?
- How do you pass on your experience to others?
- How do you continue to learn? Who from?
- What's the biggest mistake you ever made?
- What's your approach to decision making? What are the main influencing factors?
- Would you describe yourself as lucky?

This list should not be slavishly followed – a good facilitator will adapt these and perhaps insert others which are specific to the guest.

What is actually happening in a storytelling session is that people are equipped to look through another person's eyes, and when faced with a decision, be able to consider the question 'What would *** do'? In effect, these events are all about repertoire broadening in all its aspects; insights are shared, developing people's vision and their appreciative ability. Guests talk about what they did – and the audience's repository of potential options for action is deepened. Successes and failures are described and analysed, and thus the set of constraining values is made more mature.

In order to make sure that the maximum benefit is derived from the evening, it is strongly recommended that a debrief session is held within a couple of days of the evening to discuss what you learned from the event. This provides time for reflection, sharing and discussion of the various ideas raised, and allows people to consider how best to modify/implement these ideas in their own area. A typical 'morning after' comment would be '*I don't exactly know what I learned, but I do know I've never ever learned as much in just a couple of hours*'. Over time, some condensed 'wisdom' output from these sessions may be published or included in the Learning Library.

The first time people attend one of these events, they are likely to be a little uncomfortable with their unstructured nature and lack of defined task or desired outcome. The facilitator should address this in her/his opening remarks, but it will also be necessary to watch for and steer the more task-oriented delegates away from attempting to impose structure at various points throughout the evening. Promoting and establishing the benefit and reputation of these events across the wider organisational world should help in managing the expectation of such delegates away from the 'never mind the facts, just gimme the answer' management culture.

Stories by the fireside can be run at many differing levels – they do not need to just be restricted to senior management or soon-to-retire guests. Equally, the above scenario may not always be possible or appropriate. It should be adapted to the situation. Even just getting a few people round a table informally can deliver amazing insights.

Tours of the unfamiliar

These are a particularly suitable type of event for younger 'fast track' recruits, allowing them to capture learning and experience from 'outside' organisations – either internal business units with a different culture and tradition, or external, unconnected organisations from different market sectors. In many cases, part of the learning experience is in dispelling the myth of uniqueness; that in fact, businesses with very different products have identical problems.

A tour of the unfamiliar involves exactly that – delegates from different parts of the business meet centrally, and join a bus which takes them to their various workplaces – and on arrival at each, the 'home' delegate presents a short case study of a recent project, which is then followed by a discussion aimed at identifying the key issues. The commonality of such issues across the varying projects, which appear initially dissimilar, offers an opportunity for the establishment of a foundation set of core PM problems situations which will always need to be addressed irrespective of the type of deliverable.

Tours of the unfamiliar are not simply study tours although they might take the above form, the concept can also be applied to secondments at an individual level (rather like the growing practice of big football clubs putting their future star players out on loan to smaller clubs to give them experience which simply could not be gained in the heat of the Premiership).

It is important to note that in order to extract maximum benefit from such visits, they cannot be allowed to just stand alone, but must be fully debriefed and the learning recorded in the Learning Library. Additionally, such activities and subsequent reflection must be seen as part of the overall leadership responsibility to develop the competencies of their team. Much of this will be based upon leaders teaching by example, devoting time to making sure that team members understand the thought processes behind the decision making they have observed, and taking every opportunity to include junior team members in a wide range of activities to broaden their experiences and helping them reflect afterwards. One particularly good example of this in one of our client business teams is the regular inclusion of graduates in customer/supplier meetings as an observer, in order to give some exposure to the broad project context. The point here is not just that this is being done – the more significant point is the leader's initiative and concern for team development in making the most of whatever opportunities present themselves.

Libraries with Legs

While it is true that age and experience do not always go hand in hand – 'greybeards' sometimes turn out not to have 30 years' experience, but one years' experience repeated 30 times – there is a huge stock of real wisdom that every year, gold watch in hand, walks out of the door into retirement and is lost forever, whiling away its time playing golf while the next generation repeats the same mistakes.

A 'Library with Legs' is a register of areas in which people feel that they have built up a significant body of experience (and thus established and extended their repertoire) in various areas of work. When other teams are presented with new projects, tools and/or techniques containing elements with which they are unfamiliar, they can access the 'library' of experienced people, who will be able to tell them not just the basic principles of a new technique or approach, but also tell them stories of 'what happened when I tried it'; the pitfalls; the real (as opposed to claimed) advantages and so forth, perhaps staying in contact to act in some form of mentoring role as the project proceeds. Another similar technique observed in one high-achieving (and very learning-oriented) team, is termed a 'Committee of Taste'. In this, a group of very experienced people from differing disciplines can be called together on an ad-hoc basis to combine their joint views whenever a particularly difficult problem is faced.

Some organisations report using a similar approach, which they term 'peer assist' – at the start of a new project, the project team calls a 'peer assist' to import knowledge from others and from past projects.

At the end, a 'retrospect' enables the team to make conscious, capture and codify new accumulated knowledge for future use.

Wisdom costs a lot of time and money to build, but once gained, it is too valuable an asset to waste. The opportunity to share it and add it to the organisational and individual repertoire should be taken whenever it presents itself.

The project diary

There are two different aspects that must be considered with regard to learning capture during project execution.

First, it is necessary to capture what actually happened – the 'facts'. This is rarely as easy as it sounds; unless every single event is rigorously recorded at the time, it is inevitable that different people will remember things differently, putting their own interpretation on what happened, forgetting some details and embellishing others. Once the 'facts' have been recorded, the even more difficult part is extracting their significance – the relationship between cause and effect is usually complex. This issue is dealt with later, in the discussion of Learning Histories .

The clear answer to the problem of capturing the immediate facts of an event is the maintenance of a detailed and comprehensive event diary – possibly on an individual basis, though ideally a common one to which all major actors have access and authority to contribute. There will always be a difference between individual views and priorities, resulting in a subjective influence to diary entries – better if this is explicit and subject to discussion rather than left unsaid and action taken on the basis of misinterpreted or incorrect assumption. However, to maintain such a diary demands a strong self-discipline, which is rarely sustained, especially when under time/resource pressure. Unfortunately this will be when an accurate record is probably going to be most needed.

The project diary will not just contain formal meeting minutes; it should also record informal conversations, decisions made, and the reason for those decisions in the face of alternative approaches. This is especially important when the team composition changes; previous decisions may appear totally mysterious in the absence of contemporary context.

'Lessons learned' reports

A number of organisations generate 'lessons learned' reports as a matter of course, and often an organisation's Lifecycle Management process will mandate their production at phase end. Unfortunately, this is largely a wasted effort – 'Lessons Captured' would be a more realistic title. In the absence of a central learning repository, containing lesson captured reports filed against an agreed set of topic keywords, and readily accessible via a suitable retrieval mechanism, it is usually difficult and often impossible to find material relevant to a task-at-hand in the timeframe in which it is needed – so people don't bother.

Additionally, the lack of a standard format means that each report varies in depth and content, making it virtually impossible to extract common lessons (which could then be incorporated into good practice/ process guidelines). A better approach would be the use of the Leaning History technique described below.

Learning Histories

A more usable method of capturing the lessons from a completed project will be the production of a 'Learning History'. This is a specific type of case study designed to gain a comprehensive view of the facts of an event by eliciting views, opinions and memories across as wide a range of participants as possible, at all levels within the organisation – and this is where accurate, contemporary project diaries make a huge contribution. Based on the principle that *'only everyone can know the truth',* the individual stories are brought together by a facilitator, who produces an uncommented timeline of events. This first draft is then circulated to all interviewees in order that factual inaccuracies can be corrected. The next stage is to highlight areas of disagreement or incongruence, identifying recurrent themes, posing questions and in particular, raising 'undiscussable' issues. It would usually be the case that this initial analysis is performed by an independent assessor who has an appropriate level of experience in the type of event under consideration. At the end, a comprehensive, commented history records both the project timeline and the issues that arose.

LEARNING HISTORY WORKSHOPS

The commented Learning History then forms the basis of a learning workshop. The facilitator leads the group through a series of conversations based on the highlighted areas and attempts to draw out their lessons, thus allowing the group to reflect on a collective basis bringing the possibly hidden (either intentionally or unconsciously) significance of each of these issues to the surface. It is very important that participants feel relaxed and encouraged to be open and honest about their opinions – one of the facilitator's main tasks is to attempt to prevent defensive attitudes from disguising the truth and preventing real learning. To this end, 'outsiders' – either to the team or to the organisation – need to be carefully briefed and all participants must be fully prepared to accept strict 'Chatham House' rules. The workshop output is then added to the Learning History document set.

After the workshop – and with the agreement of all the participants – Learning Histories may subsequently be made available (subject to commercial confidentiality) in a learning database for access by others. Recording and retrieval methods are covered below.

What a project Learning History is not is a body of evidence to be used as a means of identifying and punishing the 'guilty' or exonerating the 'innocent'. Any such usage will very quickly bring the whole concept of Experiential Learning into disrepute, leading to a loss of both trust and value. Equally, it is only possible to learn from the past if what is recorded is factual, truthful and to the point; pasteurised accounts, or those performed for merely cosmetic purposes, are a complete waste of time and can be dangerously misleading. If a Learning History risks being edited, censored or otherwise bowdlerised for so-called 'confidentiality' purposes, there is really no point in expending the effort in producing it.

Learning validation

In every case where 'lessons' are captured, they must be validated before recording and dissemination. It may be that the conclusions are simply wrong; they may be too subjective; possibly misinterpreted; that they have been 'spun' for political reasons; obsolete, or superseded by technology.

The Learning History workshop process is a good validation mechanism; in the absence of this or similar, at the very least lessons and conclusions should be reviewed by an independent subject matter expert before being entered into the Learning Library.

On completion of validation, the learning should be recorded in the Learning Library at two levels – an abstract or brief overview, describing the Learning History content in no more than about 250 words, in order that browsers may immediately asses relevance to their current issues; and a full history, either as one document or in a more sophisticated form, further analysed and categorised according to the similarity types described above.

In both cases, they should include the contact details of a history 'owner', to whom requests for further information should be made.

Learning recording and retrieval

In order that the maximum leverage can be gained from the production of Learning Histories and lessons, common filing and retrieval methods are necessary components of the Learning Library; an organisational 'Dewey Decimal' system is essential, using a common set of keywords to describe the main issues and allow future retrieval for similarity analysis. These fall into four main groups:

- Customer(s): This needs to be a little more specific than simply the organisation name – for example, 'Ministry of Administrative Affairs', or 'ACME Engineering International' should be expanded to offer more detail and identify possible similarities; customer keywords should at least include division and department, where relevant.
- Supplier(s): As for customers, to the same depth.
- Project deliverable: Bridge, Vehicle, Control System, Technology or Service.
- Lifecycle Phase: It may be that the history covers only one lifecycle phase, or spans several. Even though by and large what happens in each phase is contingent on decisions made in previous phases, it is recommended that only the phase(s) directly addressed in the history are used as keywords.

These keywords may be used to perform an initial search of the Learning Library, allowing retrieval of learning from past projects – 'What products have we delivered to Customer A?' 'Were there any problems in agreeing the Requirements Specification with Supplier X?'.

Simulation and scenarios

> *Military strategy must be understood as a system of options since only the beginning of a military operation is plannable. As a result, the main task of military leaders consists in the extensive preparation of all possible outcomes.*
>
> *Feldmarschal Helmuth Von Moltke*

It would be rare for a significant new ship, aircraft, land vehicle or any other major system not to go through a significant degree of prototyping, modelling and simulation before a final design is agreed. The Systems Approach to projects suggests that the same is true; and that simulation, or scenario modelling, can be a significant learning experience, helping people be prepared for a number of eventualities, if not all possible outcomes.

There are two main types of Scenario Workshop. Based on past events, at the simplest level, they need be little more than a working through of a Learning History with accompanying discussion; but a much better approach, if it can be arranged, we term an '*If I had been you*' session. A timelined scenario is presented by a facilitator, based on a real-life past project. At critical points, where a decision had to be made, the presentation is paused, and workshop attendees invited to discuss what would be their decision in that circumstance. On completion of the first discussion, (and best if it can be a surprise) the actual Project Manager joins the group, hears their opinion on what they would have done, tells them what he or she actually did, and whether in hindsight their approach would have been better. The Project Manager then takes over from the facilitator, tells the next instalment of the story, and at each subsequent decision point gives the group the opportunity to talk through their suggested choices before again explaining what actually was done. Our experience of such workshops is that the Project Manager often enjoys as much if not more learning than the delegates themselves; the opportunity for such informed in-depth reflection-on-action rarely presents itself.

Scenarios which present possible future events can be even more instructive, and in fact this technique is ancient. Usually referred to as the Case Method, or perhaps 'If p then what?', it was used by Aristotle when teaching Alexander the Great and his friends; Julius Caesar and Napoleon Bonaparte were believers; Harvard Business School and many prestigious other educational organisations consider it to be by far the most effective way of educating potential top management. The facilitator/educator, who should be a highly experienced practitioner of unquestioned credibility, posits a future situation, possibly informed by current risk analysis, (although not necessarily so – the bizarre/unexpected happens all too often and therefore 'off-the-wall' scenarios should not be excluded). In the ensuing discussion, all sides of the argument are investigated. A useful additional technique for this is 'Socratic Dialectic' – where opposing arguments are presented by people who do not necessarily hold that opinion themselves – the principle behind the English Parliamentary system of 'loyal opposition'. Arguing from the other side is a technique which, once learned, allows great insight into the complexities of a given situation.

Personal and organisational learning

This is the non-project-specific aspect of learning activity. Personal learning increases individual repertoire in order that he or she may apply their own and others experience to problems at hand and make better informed decisions; it also contributes to personal development and growth as people progress in their career. Personal learning is complemented by the repertoire of all the people within that organisation. It may be that an individual problem owner does not themself need to possess the relevant knowledge and/or wisdom, so long as someone else in the organisation does, and that the problem owner knows they do and has access to it. Establishing and developing individual repertoire will be dependent on the role that particular individual plays or wishes to play in the future; but additionally, it is also necessary to define the overall knowledge and wisdom needs of the current and future organisation, ensure that these exist in nominated individuals, and establish clear communication paths to them.

Transfer of personal learning is the way an organisational repertoire grows, and vice versa (Figure 6.7); but it doesn't happen automatically. In organisations where mutual trust is low, people may be reluctant to share what they have learned; they will feel that knowledge is power,

Figure 6.7   The personal learning repertoire

and that sharing it may reduce their value to the point where they are no longer needed. Wisdom is gained over time; all too often, we let it walk out of the door, perhaps even paying it to go, when early retirement or voluntary redundancy is offered to the longer-serving (and probably most expensive) members of the workforce. These are the Libraries with Legs mentioned earlier – hugely valuable assets, and letting their knowledge go unrecorded is an utter waste, not to mention a mark of disrespect. In our experience, provided they are given adequate recognition and feel secure in their role, the majority of wise practitioners get a high degree of personal satisfaction from sharing their accumulated wisdom; as mentioned earlier, the vehicle of story is particularly good at transferring lessons, and such people have many stories to tell. Stories don't even have to be factual to convey truth; the odd embellishment actually serves to make the story more interesting and memorable. For countless centuries, parable, myth and legend have been the vehicle for passing on wisdom from generation to generation, with the young sitting around a fireside at the feet of their elders, eager to hear and learn. Nowadays we have PowerPoint. And thrusting, high-potential, Blackberry-toting executives who are far too busy to listen to some old buffer droning on. Oscar Wilde: '*I am not young enough to know everything.*'

Through-life learning

The learning priorities, and the timing of the above learning tools and techniques, will vary from project to project – the pre-PCM referred to earlier will identify the gaps in capability and inform learning planning. In general terms, however, Figure 6.8 shows typical Experiential Learning activity across the lifecycle.

Learning visions

Organisational Experiential Learning costs money; and the return is not easy to measure, since it would necessitate measuring the number of bad things that don't happen as a result of an institutionalised Experiential Learning process. Counting the absence of errors can only be done by comparison with the expected result of doing nothing

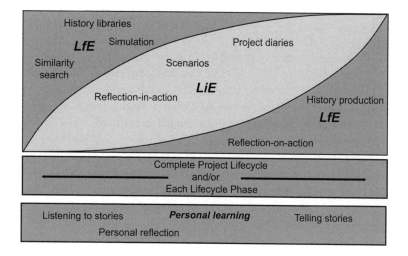

Figure 6.8   Typical Experiential Learning activity

by projecting from past failure rates; and as most organisations are in denial about the cause of such difficulties, blaming anything other than their own lack of Experiential Learning, the task is probably not worth trying.

Instead, learning effectiveness should be seen as the achievement of the organisational learning vision – the desired future reality, as described earlier – and this learning vision is multifaceted. An example might be as below:

- We will never make the same mistake twice – which means we need to recognise what a mistake is, openly accept that mistakes have been made, diagnose their cause and change our process in order to eliminate the possibility of the mistake being repeated.
- We will recreate successes.
- We will diagnose success with as much rigour as we diagnose failure, and institutionalise the process that created it. Which doesn't mean just doing the same thing – what worked once might not work next time if external circumstances have changed.

- If one person in the organisation knows it, every person in the organisation can know it.
- We will provide organisation-wide access to a library of knowledge, skill and wisdom, the development and maintenance of which is a fundamental organisational priority.
- We will remember how to do things. And we will teach the next generation so that the knowledge isn't lost when we go home.
- We will know what to do next. Because we will recognise patterns and we will have practiced.
- We will be prepared for the unexpected. Because we will have thought through and tried to identify risks and possibilities.
- AND because we will have learned things which, although they didn't seem relevant at the time, have added to our repertoire and give us the capability and confidence to improvise.

Organisational resistance/learning barriers

No one ever argues that Experiential Learning is a bad thing to do, or denies its benefits. Unfortunately, though, it is rare to see it assiduously or comprehensively performed, even in those organisations where complex projects are the norm. There are a number of reasons for this.

Leadership impatience – *'just gimme the answer, don't confuse me with options'* denies the opportunity for debate and reflection before commitments are made. When combined with unrealistic and unjustified optimism – *'I know we've always had problems and delays before, but this time it'll be different'* and simple pig-headed arrogance, *'I wouldn't have got to the where I am today if I wasn't already good at everything – there is nothing I can possibly learn'* it is unlikely that investment in learning will be a priority. This is exacerbated by the difficulty in measuring the benefits, and the fact that the investment is front-loaded but the reward may take time to emerge. If the elapsed time between the decision to invest and the point where the benefit outweighs cost exceeds the Mean Time

Between CEOs, or Government Ministers in the case of the public
sector, it is highly unlikely that the funds will be made available – it
would need a philanthropically-minded leader to invest bottom-line
money from this year to the benefit of their successor, and you don't
get many of them around here.

It also demands a great deal of faith to defend the learning
programme when the boss asks how much you've spent and what
you've delivered when you're halfway through, blown most of the
cash and haven't got much to show for it yet. I've been there, and
it ain't pleasant. Figure 6.9 is actually characteristic of all major
improvement programmes, not just learning. But through the long,
dark night of the soul, St John of the Cross tells us that we can be
encouraged by *'the spark, bright and blue as steel, glittering with
the steady light of some distant star in the frosty sky of Winter, that
dissipates the darkness'*. We shall be justified in the end – let us hope
we'll still be around to see it.

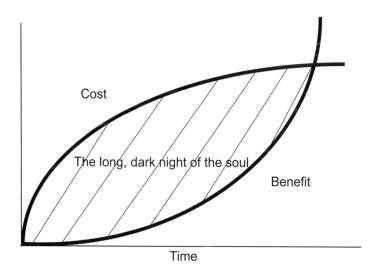

Figure 6.9   The long dark night of the soul

There are personal barriers as well. A person who feels insecure in their position in the organisation will tend to feel that knowledge is power, and be reluctant to share, squirreling away what they know as a defence mechanism. Fear of blame will prevent the truth of past mistakes being revealed; false memory syndrome will amplify and distort the past, leading to incorrect interpretation of past lessons; and the desire to stay within a comfort zone will prevent obsolete knowledge from being discarded from the repertoire.

The way to combat these barriers is the same as enacting any significant process change: early quick wins to demonstrate the benefits; good communication of purpose; continuous communication of progress – good or bad; comprehensive stakeholder involvement from the outset; and above all, leadership (again).

CHAPTER 7

APPROPRIATE CONTRACTING[1]

The universe never did make sense; I suspect it was built on government contract.

Robert A. Heinlein

A verbal contract isn't worth the paper it is written on.

Samuel Goldwyn

The customer is your enemy.

Unattributable (but you know who you are)

The worst example of *in*appropriate contracting I ever saw was some years ago when performing an independent post-project review of a major infrastructure project, the schedule and cost of which had been announced (for politically expedient reasons) by central government before any real estimation had been undertaken, and where the customer PM team had little previous experience of anything even approaching the same size and duration. In order to preserve the schedule – which of necessity was unextendable, since the project had to be delivered on an irrevocably fixed date – unquantified cost overruns were inevitable; the prevailing attitude had been '*just get on with it – we've no time to discuss and agree the details now – we'll sort everything out afterwards. Trust us*'. The general management of both purchaser and supplier was kept in the shade, if not the dark, with project reviews showing amber at worst – somewhat understandably, since their past behaviour when told the real situation had been to

---

1   With special thanks to Tim Cummins, President and CEO of the International Association for Commercial and Contract Management (IACCM) for his advice and comments on this chapter.

simply threaten the respective project teams with increasingly painful tortures. When 'afterwards' eventually came, the main subcontractors put in significant claims for variations, which were challenged by the customer, who insisted that they were not variations at all but necessary and fundamental aspects. They admitted that these had only loosely been defined (or not defined at all) in the requirements, but they claimed that in their view the subcontractor – 'selected due to their experience and knowledge' – should have understood what would be needed, identified and addressed issues as they occurred, and anyway, sufficient contingency should have been included in the tolerances of the bid price.

The supplier maintained that to do so would have put up the cost way beyond the project budget – and anyway, their bid price had been beaten down in negotiations to a barely profitable level, completely eroding any inbuilt cost resilience. Additionally, they claimed that (despite being selected on the basis of their 'experience and knowledge') the customer had repeatedly ignored any creative suggestions for alternative, more expedient approaches they had made throughout project execution. The arbitration process concentrated entirely on prising out the exact wording of every single contract phrase, and dismissed practicalities and real-world experience as merely opinion. With the exception of the lawyers, the outcome was unsatisfactory to all parties, who went away muttering words of revenge. *They asked for an open-book project,* the subcontractor MD told me, *next time, I'll keep two sets of books – the ones I show them, and the real ones.* The customer went to great lengths to publicly criticise the subcontractor; the government equally publicly blamed the customer project team management; the newspapers blamed the government; the taxpayers ended up paying in one form or another anyway, and invoked a plague on all their houses. The fact that the system is now fully operational and delivering well in excess of the expected benefits goes unreported.

OK – I admit this wasn't one project, but an amalgam of many. But you will recognise the pattern. External, poorly informed pressure is put on the main actors to work within the constraints of an unrealistic project envelope – minimum cost, maximum functionality, quickest delivery.

The oldest engineering question in the world goes like this: '*You can have it quick, you can have it cheap, or you can have it right. Now you tell me which two out of the three you want.*'

I'm a Systems Analyst by trade, who manages projects for a living. I don't really understand money. But Appropriate Contracting isn't really about money, anyway – it's about the application of common sense to a commercial relationship, to satisfy both short- *and longer-term* objectives. The money is *not* the only currency of the transaction; the quality of the relationship itself, knowledge and skill transfer, emergent creativity and innovation– all of these work together to deliver mutually agreed success. Inappropriate contracting happens when financial aspects become more important than a fit-for-purpose outcome, and the contract works against doing the right thing; the problem is compounded when it becomes a vehicle for punishing the wicked as well. Contractual unsuitability is further exacerbated when the CoO and the desperate need for approvals overrides the unacceptable truths of a real-world situation.

The one single aspect that underpins Appropriate Contracting models is trust. And trust is a hugely difficult thing to establish. When people talk about 'earning' trust, they are demonstrating that they just don't understand its nature. You *can't* earn trust – it can only be freely *awarded*, on the basis of experience in a relationship. I cannot *demand* that you trust me – I can only demonstrate my trustworthiness by my actions, and wait in hope that trust will be constructed in the eye of the beholder over a period of time.

To make matters worse, in addition to being slow and difficult to construct, trust is also as fragile as ash: trust built up over years can be instantaneously destroyed by one single betrayal, even if accidental or unintentional.

Trust is not simply an expectation that the other party will act in one's own best interest – it is more about predictability. Major contractual issues rarely occur between parties who have long experience in dealing with each other, even if it is simply a case of the 'devil you know'. Trust is awarded when each other's strengths, weaknesses and behaviours are fully appreciated, understood and accepted. I have a friend who is a builder. I've known him for years. I trust him to do a good job at a fair price. I also trust that he is unlikely to turn up when he says he will. 'Be back in the morning' doesn't necessarily mean *tomorrow* morning. I've learned to live with it, and make my plans accordingly. He's always turned up eventually.

In complex programmes, it is unlikely that such relationships will have been established – extended, untested supply chains, new technologies, cultural and behavioural differences and a lack of mutual domain experience will all militate against the awarding of the requisite level of trust needed. The contract is there to provide the framework on which trust can be built; however, all too often, it serves as a barrier instead. Many times, I have heard commercial people quote Robert Frost in their negotiations: '*Good fences produce good neighbours.*' Unfortunately, they fail to realise that the poet was using irony; the contract is all too often a fence made of barbed wire and electrified for good measure. Instead, it ought to be the vehicle which allows the fence to be pulled down; the real point of the poem is that good neighbours don't need fences at all.

The main casualty of mistrust is the pressure to contract too early in the lifecycle, resulting in the supplier proceeding at risk, and the customer having made a commitment to what is essentially an unknown quantity. Barry Boehm's classic *Software Engineering Economics* (1981) describes a 'cone of uncertainty', (a simplified version of which is shown in Figure 7.1) plotting estimation accuracy against lifecycle phase, and showing (from hard empirical evidence) that a project cost estimate made at the feasibility stage can be out by a factor of 4, reducing to a possibly inaccuracy factor of 1.25 *even when requirements have been agreed* – scope creep, PEST/ STEEPLED factors and stakeholder changes don't ever go away.

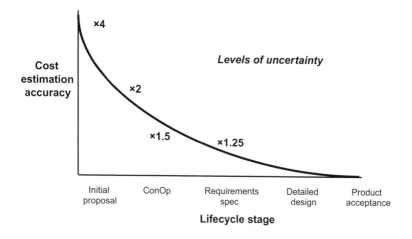

Figure 7.1   Levels of uncertainty
Source: Adapted from Barry Boehm, *Software Engineering Economics* (1981).

It is clearly ridiculous to sign a contract that sets firm, legally-binding costs and schedules until the scope and requirements are accurate and realistic; but it happens all the time. Given that most disagreements are around scope, and that scope will determine both cost and schedule, effort in assiduous scope and requirements validation is not just a wise, but a mandatory investment.

The bid process itself should be seen as the vehicle for this – it can be a highly effective complexity attenuator when viewed as a pan-stakeholder data/idea collection exercise. It can identify uncertainty and inform all parties about the validity of the assumptions behind the estimates they will work with, and the likely issues emerging throughout the project execution. Additionally, although it has been said often that the only time you know the cost and duration of a project is when it has been delivered, in truth, you don't – post-delivery costs including fault correction, maintenance, support and disposal are all subject to the vagaries of implementation in the real world and should be addressed and included in the estimation process. Estimation is, by definition, imprecise; an estimate without accompanying risk-assessed boundaries can only be a guess, and guesses which form the basis of a binding agreement are dangerous to all parties. The siren-like temptation to offer and believe the cheapest, fastest proposal has to be resisted. Money 'saved' in early lifecycle stages equals cost overruns later.

This does pose a problem in a competitive tendering environment – the enquiry stage needs as many in-depth contributions as possible from all parties, and suppliers are generally unwilling to commit comprehensive experience and resource (knowing that this may assist their competitors) unless there is a high probability of winning the bid. It is a sales and marketing axiom that it is far better to be eliminated at Round One than to come runner-up on the shortlist. For this reason, the customer must give consideration to making a contribution to bid costs; under a chargeable service agreement, a wide mix of potential suppliers can offer their collective experience and domain knowledge to ensure the broadest possible enquiry into outcome, scope, and requirements definition. They are perhaps also less likely to exaggerate what they can deliver in a non-competitive information collection exercise that leads to more accurate collective estimation and allows final contracts to be delayed until the latest possible lifecycle phase, when uncertainty is at its lowest. A good example in practice would be the new St Petersburg airport – the customer held a design competition, the winning design was used as the specification, but the winner was not allowed to bid for the project. Resisting the pressure to downselect until the critical elements have been proven maximises confidence in the production schedule and operational date. The more you know, the safer you are. Francis Walsingham, Elizabeth I's spymaster general: *'Intelligence is never too dear.'*

So what does an *appropriate* contract look like? Adopting the Systems Approach discussed earlier, we must first address its fundamental purpose. According to Tim Cummins, CEO of IACCM, a contract is in essence a system to define the communication channels and ensure a mutual understanding between all parties in order to support the relationships on which successful trade depends. It must therefore:

- establish consensus and consent between the trading parties;
- ensure clarity and reduce ambiguity regarding their intent;
- allocate roles and responsibilities related to performance;
- agree mechanisms to underpin trust and confidence in working together;
- document processes and principles related to the management of success or failure.

It is important to remember that the purpose of a contract is primarily to capture and record an economic transaction. It reflects an alignment of economic interests – and the role of the contract management process is to preserve that alignment – or to recognise their misalignment and take appropriate steps (which could include termination). These economic interests will change over time, as will the constitution of the stakeholder teams. It is rare for the teams involved in the bid process to be the same team that executes and implements the project. For that reason, it is extremely important to maintain a record of the rationale behind decisions made in order that subsequent leadership can understand the intention and if necessary, adjust their plans and agreements accordingly.

There is no definitive example of an 'appropriate' contract – it all depends on the nature of the transaction. There are multiple ways that this can be segmented. Perhaps the most commonly used method within the procurement community is based on the level of spend. Unfortunately, this is generally also the least appropriate method, because it bears little direct connection to the scale of risk or opportunity, or the dependencies for a successful outcome.

First and foremost, the contract should be establishing a framework for success. This is true whether it covers an input (for example, a product acquisition), an output (for example, provision of a service), or an outcome (for example, an outsourcing arrangement). Within this framework, there are four basic elements:

1. Scope and goals – what the agreement is about.
2. Responsibilities – who does what.

3. Performance indicators – how do we know it is on track.
4. Rights and remedies – what happens if things change or performance is not met.

In terms of typical content, the first three areas typically represent between 60 per cent and 85 per cent of the contract. Yet when it comes to negotiation, it is bullet four – the rights and remedies – that represent the lion's share of time. That is because contracts have become hijacked by the risk experts, who frequently debate allocation of risk, rather than its management. Somehow, we have allowed contracts to lose their business and commercial context and instead to become fixated on issues such as liabilities, indemnities, intellectual property rights and liquidated damages.

In pure commodity acquisitions, this focus is rarely damaging because the risks are typically quite low. But as we move into services and complex projects, the consequences of hijacking what should be an economic instrument by the risk and legal communities becomes much more significant. By failing to adequately discuss and describe the areas of scope, responsibility and performance, we create an agreement that increases the probability of failure. Rather than managing risk, the contracting process itself becomes a *source* of risk.

Over 50 years ago, Professor Ian MacNeil was arguing that risk and legal precision is increasingly unreliable (MacNeil 1969), and therefore increasingly inapplicable, in proportion to the duration of the contract. What is need is 'essential' contracting; in the uncertain environment of complex projects, it is flexibility and the strength of relationships that will allow for accommodation of changing circumstances. In his 'land of post-technique', there is no such thing as a single 'best' practice, only a set of good processes which can be applied to the specifics of the prevailing contemporary situation as the contract proceeds – planning as you go along, rather than starting out with a comprehensive and exhaustive plan than departs from reality very quickly, but is still held up as truth. Like many original thinkers, however, his view has perhaps been a bit too radical to be widely accepted – it takes courage for the stakeholders of a major programme to trust each other to that degree when a distrustful and self-seeking world is watching over their shoulder. (Interestingly, in addition to being one of the world's pre-eminent scholars in the field of contract law, and one of Barack Obama's law professors, MacNeil was the 46th Chief of the Clan MacNeil, in line of descent from Niall of the Nine Hostages, High King of Ireland and 26th MacNeil of Barra. He gave the crofting estate of Barra to the Scottish nation, and granted the lease of the thousand-year-old Kisimul Castle to Historic Scotland for the next thousand years at an annual rent of one bottle of whisky – an 'essential' contract if ever there was one.)

If Complex projects are to be managed and governed under sensible, realistic contractual frameworks, the underlying, combative, practices of procurement *must* change. Supply-side practices need to accommodate reality. All parties must address the all-too-frequent breakdown in the core honesty and integrity of trading relationships, with an absence of good governance and oversight at its core. It is also necessary to introduce new thinking to risk assessment and allocation, possibly drawing on principles already embedded in the insurance industry. The critical factor is leadership that is strong enough to instigate and support collaborative action and exercise robust, appropriately targeted management of performance and behaviour, in order that contracts are rightly positioned as a tool for structuring the relationships (and perhaps infrastructures and protocols) that are robust enough to meet the inevitable uncertainties.

Essentially, the challenge is about forming the right team and gaining the right stakeholder inputs at the right time, working to build trust both externally and internally – which can often be harder. Contention is inevitable in any large organisation, but it can be creative, or it can be destructive. If there is no internal collaboration, then many of the 'internal experts' are often left out of the core term and/or introduced at the last minute. As a result, their input and ideas are omitted or ignored, chances for commercial creativity are lost, and they become 'auditors' – focused on what 'the idiots did wrong'. At this point, since no one is willing to re-open the fundamentals of the deal, they are constrained to offer only 'risk management' techniques – such as battling over liabilities and so on.

The structuring of the team and the timing of inclusion is key. Indeed, experience shows that one of the best ways to drive successful contracts is to recognise that if the relationship framework and communication paths have not been clearly defined and established prior to the bidding process, they probably will never be. Dealing with the commercial and relationship fundamentals in the heat of a bid process just doesn't work, partly due to time pressures and partly due to the competitive concerns discussed above.

*In*appropriate contracts will be here to stay until we accept – and act upon – the incontrovertible fact that achieving successful outcomes in the light of a dynamic external environment throughout both project execution and product life demands imagination, creativity, flexibility, a mutual language and continuing, unconditional trust; and that an *appropriate* contract is one, underpinned by these attributes, that addresses the issues of scope, responsibilities and performance in the delivery of that outcome rather than anticipating failure.

CHAPTER 8

CONCLUSION

Making the simple complicated is commonplace; making the complicated simple, awesomely simple, that's creativity.

Charles Mingus

So what? As we said at the beginning, if you do what you've always done, you'll get what you always get. And if what you get isn't good enough, you need to do something else. Trouble is, we are conditioned by many things – our past, our training, our language, our culture. These have become enculturalised to the point where they are articles of faith – we espouse a value set that encourages cynicism and mistrust, believes that process alone can save the planet, doesn't think that the previous generation had a clue, applies a rationalist/positivist/ empiricist philosophy and confidently expects that the external environment will enter a state of suspended animation for the whole of the project lifecycle. O brave new world! That has such people in it!

Let's imagine we are faced with a major, complex, project that has never been done before, has to succeed first time, has multiple stakeholders each with their own view of what would constitute success, must be delivered by an agreed date, cannot exceed its budget once it has been established, is highly publicly visible and which will be rigorously audited to ensure no wastage of money or resource. What would we do? (Hiding behind the sofa might appear attractive, but let us assume that option is closed to us; having said which, it may sometimes be the better option in circumstances where pride, overconfidence or eagerness to please makes us say 'yes' when invited to lead the impossible).

Before we get into the first order processes – Bid, Requirements, WBSs, OBSs, and so on, let's start with some blank pieces of paper, and write down two headings: 'Vision' and 'Values'. Vision is the statement, in the present tense, of the prevailing situation as we wish it to be on project completion, the equivalent of Cato's 'Carthago Delenda Est', as discussed earlier. Cancer *is* cured; the whole world *is* at peace; I *am* walking on Mars; we *are* the champions. The vision must be shared – and subscribed to unconditionally – by everyone who will be an actor in the project, and to that end, should be turned into a banner that is in clear line of sight from each and every desk and workbench. People can ask themselves, 'Is what I am doing making that vision reality?' – and if it isn't, they should do something else that is.

The Vision is a statement of where we finally want to be; Values describe the principles that will underpin the decisions taken on the journey. They are not vague, bland and politically correct, as so often seen in the 'Our Values' plaque in the marbled reception halls of the megacorporations. Value statements must be practical, workable, and relevant. The following example is one of the best I've seen – and one of the *very* few that I have ever experienced a project team living to.

Our Values are the rules by which we live – the filters through which we evaluate possible actions, the base upon which we make decisions in support of the achievement of our collective and individual vision and purpose.

We take good Risks. Complacency kills slowly, risk aversity kills quickly. The result, however, is the same.

We are a Team not a bunch of individuals or a group of organisations. The team is our second family. We share problems, and more significantly, we share successes.

We practice Empowerment at all levels. We accept that poor decisions are a consequence of a failure to communicate our vision, purpose and values.

We have permission to make mistakes without blame,
provided we admit them and learn from them.

We take Responsibility for our actions and those of our team.

**We accept that Internal Harmony doesn't mean agreeing with
everything.** But once a decision is made, we **Support** it totally.

We Communicate inside, outside and across,
keeping it short, sharp and to the point.

We never promise what we *know* we can't deliver. But we
are **Confident** in what we can achieve when we're stretched.

We do the Right Thing at all times no matter what.

We never tell lies... especially to ourselves.

And as a result we **Believe in ourselves and each other.**

Borrow these, modify, delete or add your own as appropriate. Then put
them on the wall everywhere the work gets done.

Once we've got Vision and Values, the next task lists the possible
lessons from everything we've done before that has similarities of
any type – structural, functional, purposive, control or relational
as described above. It's not enough just to list them, though – the
question to be addressed is what is their relevance to the task before
us, and how can we apply them?

You'll need a single-page overview that summarises the entire
adventure in simple terms, the 'elevator pitch', the Gettysburg
address, the 'pack shot', the press release, the basecamp to which you
can return when afraid of losing direction. You and others will have to
tell the story many times – it helps if the story is the same!

The attributes needed for leadership should follow – what experience, behaviours and style will be needed in the person who will create the environment in which the team will be able to deliver the vision while fending off the critics who would divert or prevent it.Even if you can't get Alexander the Great, at least you will know where the gaps are between the ideal leader and what you've got.

Next, draw the relationship map. Who needs to be able to talk to whom, and what communication channels are appropriate to their conversations? Organisational structures and protocols that stop a supplier engineer from talking to a customer engineer directly are usually symptoms of a lack of trust – or worse, a fear that they might let slip a politically or commercially unacceptable truth. Even more dangerous than that are the internal hierarchical barriers that delay – or even completely prevent – the boardroom knowing what's happening on the shop floor, and vice versa.

Finally, you need to establish where the off switch is. With the best will in the world, and the best management, some projects will go so far off track that they need to be terminated. The external environment may change, a radical new technology may arrive, you may discover that the basic understanding of the problem situation was wrong, an uncertainty may turn into a showstopping reality. It would be foolish to get into a racing car and floor the throttle if you don't know where the brake is, just as it would be to invade a country without having thought through what you're going to do when you get there – and even more importantly, how you'll get out.

There is nothing magical, or even complicated, about Second Order PM. In essence, it boils down to the carpenter's old tenet of 'measure twice, cut once'. Be absolutely certain where you want to go, and decide how best to get there (with alternatives in case of the main road being blocked by avalanche), before any major commitments are made and the detailed work obscures the overall picture.

And then, *and only then*, Cry Havoc! and let slip the dogs of war.

THE PROJECT LEADERS' COMMENTARY

During the writing of this book, I was privileged to talk to some of the world's best and most experienced Project Leaders. One of the attributes they showed in common was an enthusiasm to share their stories and their wisdom in order to inform the practice of others – a mark of true professionalism. Whilst I have attempted to incorporate their knowledge in the body of the text, some of their most trenchant quotes deserve to be included verbatim, in order to encourage careful reflection. For obvious reasons, they are unattributable.

'Project Management only becomes news when it's a bad news story.' The 'hero' Project Managers – those who pull projects back from the brink of disaster – aren't really the ones at the top of their profession. The real heroes are those whose projects come in unspectacularly – on time, on budget, delivering the desired outcome. Their stories are rarely told.

'People who come from well-organised, process-oriented backgrounds are not really able to understand complexity, and it's a mistake to push such people, talented as they may be, into situations demanding creativity and improvisation. It's the same in sport – Woods v. Ballesteros is a good example – and music – Clapton v. Hendrix. Talent plus lots of practice will bring great success, but never create genius.' The normal route to leadership of complex projects is progressive, increased seniority relying on starting small and delivering gradually larger projects. The problem is that this tends to promote those who

are accomplished first order practitioners, who may not possess the behavioural characteristics required for adhocratic leadership. It may be that First and Second Order PM should be seen as separate subdisciplines within the PM profession, and career development paths planned accordingly from an early stage.

'*OK, I agree that if it ain't broke, you don't fix it – but it **is** broke!*' The difficulty is getting people to *accept* that it's broke. Fear of blame, lack of mutual stakeholder trust, punitive contractual sanctions, and (perhaps most often) simple denial can lead to terminally-ill projects being kept on life support far beyond the point where recovery is possible.

'*If an organisation can't afford to get its budgets wrong, they need to accept the truth, however unacceptable. It is utter foolishness to believe that you can outsource risk.*' A way of dealing with the above is to pass the blame on to someone else. There is a tendency to feel secure behind rigorous contract conditions – '*if it goes belly-up we can sue them afterwards*' but post-failure litigation can't deliver retrospective success.

'*Even though we always get a lower performance than we expected, we are nonetheless incentivised to be optimistic.*' An Executive Management mindset that is obsessed with setting ever-increasing stretch targets ignores the concept of elastic limit. A Project Manager who takes on something he or she knows to be unrealistic and probably unachievable deserves all they get.

'*It is essential that we avoid the "sunk cost" issues – past expenditure must never affect current decisions.*' Peter Bernstein, in his excellent book *Against the Gòds* (Bernstein 1996), makes clear the fact that human nature is not so much risk averse as *loss* averse. We would sooner throw good money after bad than write off what we've already spent. The English and French Governments' refusal to cancel Concorde even though it became clear that it could never become economically viable is a well-known example of this. It can also manifest itself when an expensive feasibility study finds that a project would be unviable – there is a feeling that the money spent would have been wasted if the project were aborted.

'Achieving greatness at anything equals love plus 10,000 hours effort.' Quoted often, this is not to be taken literally – what it means is that success is always a combination of motivation and effort. Even then, however, the effort has to be accurately applied. One of the most important principles I learned as a music student is relevant to Experiential Learning generally: *'Practice doesn't make perfect. Only perfect practice makes perfect.'*

'We adopted an approach euphemistically called "Preference Engineering" – doing things in the way people would like them done, when a business case could not be made for so doing.' This can be taken two ways. On the positive side, it allows tacit wisdom – instinct, intuition and inspiration – to override explicit knowledge. Conversely, it undermines the good governance practice of validating the Return on Investment equation. In the positivist business world, wisdom can often go unregarded in the face of raw data presented as inalienable fact.

'The West focuses on the short term; in the East the opposite is true. It's down to culture, and it's almost impossible to change overnight.' One of the most influential Complexity Drivers is project size – and the bigger the project, the longer its duration and the anticipated life of the product, with ramifications about long-term emergent issues. It is very difficult to reconcile adequate consideration of such issues in a promiscuous investment environment which looks for instant return.

'Focus on outcome, and think about people.' The trouble with people is that they are expensive, bloody-minded and, unfortunately, necessary. No matter how comprehensive the toolset, its effective use is subject to the vagaries of the human condition. The Second Order leader's prime task is to constantly ensure that the effort of the people-at-hand, with their skills and behavioural preferences, *in their current mood*, is applied as closely as possible to delivering the desired outcome.

Abraham Maslow's hierarchy of human need (Maslow 1943) may be a simplistic model, but it's pretty useful as a start.

'*Human beings will always choose a route that best suits their personal experience, whether or not it best suits the task at hand.*' When addressing a new issue, we tend to operate through fixed mental models – looking for similarity to past experiences and sometimes shoehorning a 'fit' where one doesn't exist. What we're really doing is 'situating the appreciation' as opposed to 'appreciating the situation'. Again, leadership is needed here – leadership that is courageous enough to hear the opinion of others and accept that they might have a point, and disciplined enough to maintain a mind that is open to new things. '*The majority of our existing tools are based on what we see through the rear view mirror.*'

'*We still have the ability to build St Paul's Cathedral – but we probably wouldn't.*' Of all of the interview quotes, this is the most enigmatic. In the course of discussing something else, I had asked a throwaway question whether we had forgotten some of the skills of the past – using the example of the Egyptian Pyramids – no one really knows how they were built. The answer was 'yes' – but *why* probably wouldn't we? Because our culture doesn't allow for non-functional, purely aesthetic additions? Because we'd never get planning permission? Because we have better ways of building? Because we'd never get the funding? The discussion moved on, I didn't pursue the point and haven't had opportunity to do so since. I wish I had.

'*"Lean" doesn't work with complex projects – you need resource redundancy.*' By definition, complex projects are unpredictable. If we know exactly what we have to do, and have the known capability to do it, we can plan to the last detail with a high degree of confidence in our estimates. 'Lean' is a great first order concept. It is potentially disastrous when shall have to address the unknown unknowns.

'*The system is designed to produce the outcomes we're getting. We consistently use the low bid price as the basis of the budget. When it all goes wrong, we should ask ourselves "What did you expect?"*'

We won't, though. We shall look for other causes and explanations, and we shall do exactly the same next time. One of the visions of a good Experiential Learning programme is 'We will never make the same mistake twice.' This tends to attract two different responses. One of them is 'We shouldn't *make* mistakes at all!'. This sort of comment merely reflects the stupidity of the speaker. The other – made by people who actually *do* know what they're talking about – is 'We'd be happy if we could reduce the number of times we make the same mistake down to double figures.'

'*In reality, Liquidated Damages (LD) drive bad behaviour – they are used as a financial recovery tool, but you'll have paid extra to get them. If contracts are punitive, they will result in a loss–loss situation – a combination of poor service to the customer and financial pain for the supplier.*' Imagine a situation where significant daily LDs will be applied if you, as project Manager, don't release the product to factory acceptance testing on a contractually-agreed date. You know of a slight enhancement which will take a couple of days to implement, but doing so would mean that you miss the date and the LDs would kick in. If, however, you release the product and implement the enhancement later, it will necessitate regression testing taking three or four weeks, but you could charge the customer for this. It is not operationally critical – will simply result in slightly reduced performance under rare circumstances. The choice is yours.

'*Our priorities are cost, schedule, resources – when really we should be thinking first about relationships, infrastructure and ways of working.*' The latter are ways of delivering the former. The former can't deliver the latter.

'*Attempts to deal with complexity get strangled because the leadership hasn't the appetite for the fight – we get audited at a first order level, so that's what we make sure we do.*' We often hear people say 'If you can't measure it, you can't manage it', or alternatively 'What gets measured gets done'. In practice, imposing rigorous measures results in behaviours based only on achieving those measures, whether or not they are appropriate. You'd better make damn sure you choose the right metrics, then. Albert Einstein: '*Not everything that counts can be counted; and not everything that can be counted counts.*'

USING THE SYSTEMS ANATOMY – A CASE STUDY

THE PROBLEM SITUATION

The Anatomy approach was developed to produce an organisational strategy, project plan and supporting organisational design for a major restructuring of a long-standing business activity. While this organisation had been extremely successful in the past, its design was considered to be increasingly inappropriate in the light of both contractual and environmental changes. A majority of the executive Board however, had been working in this environment for several years and despite their verbal acceptance of the need for change, carried a significant amount of legacy 'baggage' This was combined with a slight uneasiness about anything 'academic' or 'philosophical' – the company has a strong 'Hard Engineering' ethos established over many years.

In the light of their research into existing methods, the developers felt strongly that a transformational approach based on Systems Thinking was needed; the business has complex stakeholder relationships – both formal and informal – and has to operate under externally-imposed constraints which were clearly not widely understood (or even accepted) by some of the Management team. This Systems-based approach was championed by a newly-appointed Board member, who had joined from a different business unit (therefore carrying no cultural 'baggage') and been given the responsibility to integrate and lead two previously separate functions.

CANDIDATE METHODS

There were a number of candidate methods within the Systems discipline. Peter Checkland's SSM (Checkland 1981; Checkland and Scholes 1990) had been used many times by one of the developers in consultancy assignments. However, it had never readily been accepted by senior client management. It was regarded as too 'soft and fluffy' – the concept of rich pictures was not well received by people accustomed to detailed, highly precise engineering drawings who were unused to thinking pictorially and unhappy with broad themes. However the strength of SSM in systemic enquiry and identification of stakeholder[1] viewpoints and desired transformations would clearly be hugely useful in the design process.

Alongside the strengths of SSM, Stafford Beer's VSM (Beer 1985) offered a means of understanding and balancing strategy; managerial control and communication; and operational activities against the constraints imposed by the system environment. Beer's maxim *'Absolutum Obsoletum'* – 'If it works it's out of date' seemed particularly apropos in the given problem situation. But one look at the VSM diagram, or exposure to Beer's somewhat idiosyncratic style, would have had the Board running for cover.

IDEF modelling was also considered; but although rigorously structured and pretty much comprehensive, its focus tends to be upon the functions, activities or processes *within* the modelled system with much less emphasis on external constraints and (especially) risk.

It was also felt that such a detailed, rigorous model would be a temptation to 'get down in the weeds' rather than address the issue at a broad, system level.

There were also a number of practical constraints upon the selection and design of the approach.

---

1   In SSM terminology, Stakeholder is referred to as 'Customer'.

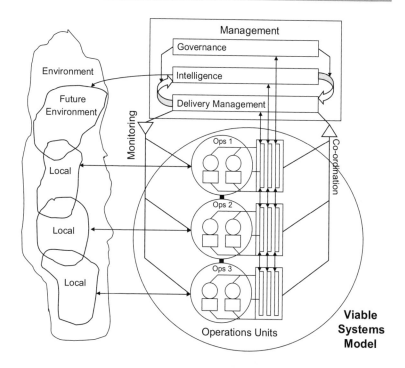

Figure A2.1   Viable Systems Model of Stafford Beer
Source: VSM diagram © Hoverstadt, P. Used with permission.

To gain views from the widest possible perspective, it was felt that the process would need to be applied in a workshop environment – individual interviews not providing the opportunity for discussion and clarification that is one of the great strengths of SSM, allowing for progress in establishment of a group perspective. In order to achieve commonality of results across different subsystems, the method needed to be easily explainable at the workshop itself (it being unrealistic to expect people to have read up on it beforehand), and usable by a number of different facilitators or even by self-facilitated groups.

It was important to dispel any entrenched negative attitudes to 'tree-hugging' workshops or 'consultants' per se. This had been evident many times when dealing with senior colleagues in previous events. There appeared to be an underlying belief in the inevitability of arriving at the desired solution without any facilitation or the use of process/methods. '*Of course the exercise was useful but people would have come to the same conclusion eventually anyway.*' This belief is hard to substantiate and equally difficult to disprove; but getting to the right conclusion 'eventually' will usually be too late for the needs of the business.

The upshot of the above was the design of an approach which incorporated the thinking behind SSM, VSM and IDEF, retaining the advantages of each while accommodating the above constraints – in other words, developing a 'light' method which could be applied with a reasonable chance of success. The term 'System Anatomy'[2] was chosen using the usual method for naming things.

SYSTEM ANATOMIES – GENERAL PRINCIPLE

Systems Anatomy Modelling offers a way of developing deeper understanding of an organisation, by treating it as a System with a clearly defined and explicit Vision and *Purpose*. Every System will have multiple Stakeholders, each with their own individual view of both the system purpose and the means by which successful achievement of this purpose will be measured. The combination of these defines the overall purpose, which will demand a number of *Activities*, each requiring Material and Capabilities at a quantified *Resource* level. The wider *Environment* will give rise to both Risk and Constraints upon the activities performed.

The generic Anatomy model is shown graphically in Figure A2.2.

---

2   **Anatomy**: (Gr. *anatomia* – to divide up). The science of the structure of organised bodies; detailed examination or analysis – *the anatomy of a crime* (OED).

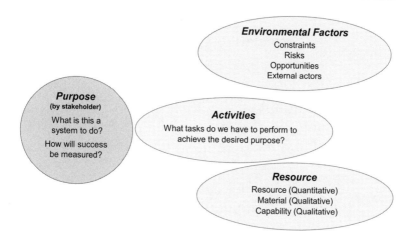

Figure A2.2   Generic Anatomy model

The business groups/projects/activities within the system are regarded as interacting components (Subsystems) which must all demonstrate a clear contribution to the achievement of this purpose – if they can't, their validity comes under serious question. In effect, the defined activities of any given system constitute the purpose of its lower-level subsystems.

Equally, the system needs to be understood as a contribution to the achievement of the purpose of a *higher* level Supersystem to which it is itself a subsystem, and from which its own purpose is derived.

The relationships between systems at each level can be represented graphically as shown in Figure A2.3.

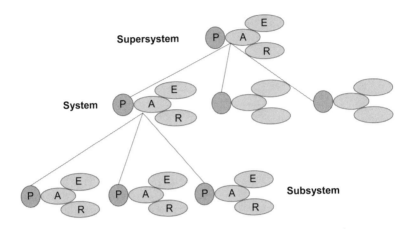

Figure A2.3 System relationships

THE SYSTEM ANATOMY WORKSHOP PROCESS

In a workshop environment, participants articulate and agree a shared system vision, identify the purpose of the system as seen from multiple stakeholder viewpoints, then derive a statement of purpose which accommodates these as widely as possible while achieving that vision. Measures of success are also determined for each stakeholder purpose. Any incompatibility between purposes is noted as risk, to be considered in later discussion. On completion, the list may be pared down to a manageable number of major stakeholders, but only if absolutely necessary. Ideally, the consideration of different viewpoints should be unrestricted – it is important to know who's going to be upset and what the longer-term consequences of this might be should they become more significant later on!

Delegates then identify, discuss and agree a list of Activities necessary to meet the accommodated purpose; these are considered in the context of their wider environment, with all its accompanying Risks and Constraints. An Owner is allocated to each activity. On completion of these elements, Qualitative discussion follows to determine the

Material and Capabilities required for successful execution of system activities.

Under normal circumstances, each activity owner should then commit to post-workshop action to derive Quantified Resource estimates based on the Material and Capability requirements.

On completion of the System Anatomy at any level, the activities derived become the subject of analysis themselves, using exactly the same approach. In effect, they become the purposes of the lower-level systems. The modelling is recursive; a guide to when analysis should stop is when the system activity is amenable to being documented as a process.

The relationships between subsystems are then mapped, and the results used to inform the production of subsystem Schematics[3] showing channels of communication and material delivery combined with support, encouragement, monitoring and control mechanisms. Again, these schematics are recursive, ranging from the system level down through its subsystems; production can continue until it is possible to produce an entity relationship diagram that may be used as part of the process documentation. These schematics may adopt several different views as appropriate; organisation charts, project plans, value and supply chains may all be derived from the anatomy models, which provide the deep level of understanding of the system on which these need to be based if they are to reflect practice rather than speculation.

In the case of Project Organisational hierarchies, is extremely important to preserve decision-making autonomy at the lowest possible subsystem level. This is the principle of Subsidiarity – *that a central governing body will permit its member states, branches, local offices, and so on to have control over those issues, decisions, actions, and so on that are most informed at, and appropriate to, that level.*

---

3   Essentially, these are Entity Relationship Diagrams, but again the terminology was felt to be a little obscure and off-putting for the workshop populations.

This principle is fundamental to the construction of an efficient and effective overall Programme Design. It would normally be the case that the activity owner would be the decisionmaking authority within that activity. Using the System Anatomy approach, identifying these activity owners turned out to be a very straightforward task.

DEPLOYING THE RESULTS

Experience showed that the workshops were virtually always well-received, with enthusiastic participation. It's the subsequent steps that were the hardest. Without strong and committed leadership prepared to communicate the results widely, accepting and accommodating feedback and then visibly supporting and encouraging implementation of the indicated changes throughout the inevitable issues arising in a managed transformation, all that would have happened is that workshop delegates would have participated in an intellectual exercise with no recognisable outcome, thereby discrediting the process itself.

In practice, this means that the Anatomy process must be itself not just sponsored, but owned, by that leadership. It cannot be applied by an external function such as strategy, business improvement or consulting – although experience proved that to remain objective, it would usually need to be externally facilitated.

PRACTICAL CONSIDERATIONS

The process developed incrementally in a series of workshops through which elements of the basic methodology were refined to deal with the challenges of using it in practice. These refinements were prompted by a number of observations and indicated improvements.

It is important to carefully manage representation of the output data and the process of interpretation and analysis in order to agree meaningful action. The complexity of the system is a function of the number of subsystems included within the system boundary and their level of interconnection. Some studies included a very large number of close-coupled subsystems initially resulting in an overwhelming amount data to be analysed and coordinated. This led to the development of a Microsoft Access database which allowed for report production and analysis of different views as well as creating a permanent record of workshop output. Additionally, it was necessary to limit the number of subsystems covered in each workshop by grouping these wherever possible. As a general rule, it was found best to restrict the number of subsystems to no more than five or six. This did have the spin-off benefit of focussing thought on what was a real subsystem, and what were actually sub-subsystems, and in practice delivered much clearer results.

It is important to identify super-system interfaces and subsystems not within the control of the problem owner in order to define the constraints that may impact on any proposed purpose. A major issue identified here was that in the absence of a clear statement and accommodated alignment of vision,[4] individual groups merely assumed their own, and these sometimes proved to be idiosyncratic and mutually incompatible. This was exacerbated by the fact that some subsystem workshops were held before the higher-level system workshop, so purposes and activities were not properly cascaded down; in fact often they went upwards. A true shared vision should act not just as a guide for action, but as a motivating and unifying factor. In the light of this experience, later workshops began with reiteration and discussion of the supersystem vision, although this was frequently modified as the enquiry process continued and a broader understanding gained.

The attachment of individuals to their current activities should also not be underestimated. Groups have a tendency to rearrange the deckchairs identifying only the activities they know and love in order to deliver the desired purpose – and if they can't, the purpose itself is what tends to be modified. The threat of the weakening

---

4   Which in the study under discussion was prevented by external political and commercial constraints.

(or even disappearance) of their position in the organisation should their activities be no longer required will inevitably influence their behaviour even if only subconsciously. This strong emotional attachment to the current understood purpose of the system will influence the groups' ability to identify – and even much less accept – any purpose which is radically different to that which it is now. The difficulty of looking at the purpose of the organisation in conceptual terms the first time it is tried is understandable, but unacceptable. The reality of how things *have been*, or even how they *are*, must never be allowed to prejudice the identification of how things *could* – and even more importantly, *should* – be.

The length of time the group have been in post will also limit the breadth of stakeholder identification and the ability to demonstrate the empathy required to understand each stakeholder's view of the system purpose[5] especially where these have changed over time. It was found that groups would quickly revert to seeing the customer community (and perhaps their own Head Office) as the only external stakeholders – sometimes including their suppliers but requiring much more prompting to include inclusion of wider (but nonetheless valid) connections, for example governments competitors and the media (an inevitable, and normally antagonistic, stakeholder in major programmes).

Attention must be paid to development of required facilitation skill sets in order to deliver meaningful outputs that motivate, encourage and support the participants in taking proactive ownership of the situation. As the workshop process spread, it became apparent that Facilitators needed a relatively high level of skill and confidence to encourage and challenge senior participants to 'park' their current view of the situation and explore other possibilities. Without this understanding, and the strength to control the workshop delegates and keep them aligned to the process, some workshops were hijacked by strong-minded delegates exercising their seniority; they consequently delivered little that was new – rather, the fact that a workshop had

---

5   That is, their 'Weltanschauung'.

taken place was claimed as evidence in support of the pre-existing views, making it harder to implement the subsequent organisational and process changes.

It became very clear that the facilitators need a sound grasp of the underlying principles of the methods and models – SSM, VSM & IDEF – upon which the Anatomy process was based, if they are to have sufficient flexibility to respond to the differing behaviours, experience and of the workshop delegates. People at senior levels in organisations will inevitably challenge any new or unfamiliar process, and unless this is met and satisfactorily addressed, little or no progress will be made – and worse, the validity of the approach will be damaged, resulting in the output of other workshops being rejected or ignored.

REFLECTION

Reflecting upon the above experience of using Anatomy Modelling in a significant number of workshops with groups differing in seniority, discipline and role, a number of common observations emerged.

It is vitally important to establish, *and gain a real commitment to,* a workshop protocol – the rules of the game – before the Anatomy Workshop begins. The Anatomy Workshop must be seen as a journey into the unknown, with the participants (and the facilitator) accepting that they don't know what the eventual outcome will be – and being flexible enough to allow for some forays into what might appear to be blind alleys. Sometimes such routes turn out to be quite the opposite. It might appear that this opportunity for new insight is incompatible with the need for compliance with the Anatomy process, but this is not necessarily the case – as with any process or method, compliance should be with its spirit, not the letter, and modelling should be tailored to the specifics of the unique situation. Having said this, it does demand that the facilitator is equipped to exercise a 'personal mastery' over the process, steering the workshop through the process with a light touch and helping it find for itself the road that leads to Ithaka.[6]

In essence, a System Anatomy Workshop is 'a conversation with the problem situation', and conversation is largely improvisational in nature. Some people are happy with this. Many are not. The behavioural preferences of the workshop delegates will have a significant effect on the outcome, and the 'tone' of the workshop should be carefully managed to address these. Groups of Engineers were generally happy to follow the process and get to an outcome, although unhappy if this was not achieved within a set time; neither did they readily accept that there could be several equally valid answers to the same question. Some Commercially-oriented people adopted a more negotiation-based stance, trying to get to a result that accommodated the views of all parties; Sales and Marketing personnel wanted to get to the result they had previously anticipated or wished for, as did General Management. Workshop delegates from more creative disciplines – Strategy, Design – seemed to be most ready to go with the conversational flow. Since behavioural change cannot be realistically expected, it is much better for the facilitator to be prepared in advance with a knowledge of the various disciplines likely to participate, and to style the workshop accordingly. It may even be that an awareness of delegate behavioural profiles, perhaps obtained through a Myers-Briggs or similar typology, may be useful in complex or difficult situations.

Further to the above, which is essentially about the workshop process, behavioural preference will also tend to influence the motivations of the attendees towards the outcome. Some will want to get to the *right* answer, even when this does not personally suit them – others will only be happy if they get to *their* answer. A major motivation for many is not to expose their lack of knowledge in front of others – particularly if this could be used 'politically' as a sign of their weakness.

Donald Schon (1994) termed the behaviours necessary to 'the public testing of private assumptions' a 'Model II theory of action', which

---

6   A long one, full of adventure, full of discovery .

is primarily philanthropic – where '*the individual is committed to an action because it is intrinsically satisfying – not, as in the case of Model I, because it is accompanied by "...rewards or punishments"*'. His suggested strategies to achieve this are based on creating an environment of co-operation, which is rather easier said than done in the combative world of internal politics and rivalries. But at least, if the facilitator is aware that such tensions exist, they can be recognised and if necessary confronted.

The results of the workshops and subsequent analysis must be acted upon, and not second-guessed post-workshop or misapplied (whether consciously or unconsciously). It is not usually within the remit or power of the facilitator to make this happen; it comes down to ownership by the system leadership, and their faith in the process itself. When this has been present, System Anatomy Modelling has proved to be an effective and efficient strategic tool that delivers viable and appropriate organisational design in support of highly complex projects.

REFERENCES

Ackoff, R. (1999). *Ackoff's Best: His Classic Writings on Management*. New York, John Wiley & Sons.

Beer, S. (1985). *Diagnosing the System for Organizations*. Oxford, Oxford University Press.

Bernstein, P. L. (1996). *Against the Gods*. New York, John Wiley and Sons.

Boehm, B. (1981). *Software Engineering Economics*. Englewood Cliffs, NJ, Prentice-Hall.

Checkland, P. (1981). *Systems Thinking, Systems Practice*. Chichester, John Wiley & Son.

Checkland, P. and J. Scholes (1990). *Soft Systems Methodology in Action*. Chichester, John Wiley & Sons.

Csikszentmihalyi, M. (1990). *Flow: The Psychology of Optimal Experience*. New York, Harper and Row.

Friedman, M. (1970). *The Social Responsibility of Business is to Increase its Profits*. New York Times.

Gray, B. (2009). 'Review of Acquisition for the Secretary of State for Defence.' http://www.mod.uk/NR/rdonlyres/78821960-14A0-429E-A90A-FA2A8C292C84/0/ReviewAcquisitionGrayreport.pdf

MacNeil, I. (1969). 'Whither Contracts.' *Journal of Legal Education* **21**(403).

Maslow, A. H. (1943). 'A Theory of Human Motivation.' *Psychological Review* **50**(4): 370–396.

McDonald, L. (2009). *A Colossal Failure of Common Sense*. New York, Random House.

Mitroff, I. I and Linstone, H. A. (1993). *The Unbounded Mind*. Oxford, OUP.

Saynisch, M. (2010a). 'Beyond Frontiers of Traditional Project Management: An Approach to Evolutionary, Self-Organizational Principles and the Complexity Theory-Results of the Research Program.' *Project Management Journal* **41**(2): 21–37.

Saynisch, M. (2010b). 'Mastering Complexity and Changes in Projects, Economy, and Society via Project Management Second Order (PM-2).' *Project Management Journal* **41**(5): 4–20.

Schon, D. (1994). *The Reflective Practitioner*. Aldershot, Ashgate.

Senge, P. M. (1990). *The Fifth Discipline*. New York, Doubleday.

Simon, H. (1997 (4th ed.)). *Administrative Behavior: A Study of Decision-Making Processes in Administrative Organizations*. New York, The Free Press

Verma, N. (1998). *Similarities, Connections, and Systems*. Lanham, Lexington.

Vickers, G. (1965). *The Art of Judgement*, Chapman & Hall.

SOME SUGGESTIONS FOR FURTHER READING

Not all of these will seem directly relevant to the topic, but are included as repertoire-broadening and appealing to the curious mind.

Ackoff, R. L. (1999). *Ackoff's Best*. New York, Wiley.

Some iconoclastic essays dealing with the Systems Approach. Ackoff can be a bit smug and irritating at times (takes one to know one), but always challenging.

Alexander, C. (1964). *Notes on the Synthesis of Form*. Cambridge, MA, Harvard.

Although this deals with architecture, the concept of 'pattern' is very relevant to thinking about similarity.

Argyris, C. (1992). *On Organisational Learning*. Cambridge, MA, Blackwell.

The foundation text on which most subsequent discussion of experiential learning is based.

Aristotle (1925). *Nicomachean Ethics*. Oxford, Oxford University Press.

This introduces the five 'intellectual virtues': Science, which is how things work; Art, which puts things together; Intuition, which is about putting things together in the 'best/right' way; Phronesis, putting the thing in to practice; and Sophia, the ability to combine all of the previous four. In my experience, Academia does the first two, lacks (in some cases derides) intuition, and distrusts phronesis as 'impure'. The reverse is true for practitioners. The 'wise' are thus few and far between.

Ashby, W. R. (1956). *An Introduction to Cybernetics*. London, Chapman & Hall.

Another fundamental text, but difficult to read.

Csikszentmihalyi, M. (1990). *Flow: The Psychology of Optimal Experience*. New York, Harper and Row.

I've only read extracts of this, but the concept of 'flow' is so familiar that it is clearly true.

de Geus, A. (1997). *The Living Company*. London, Nicholas Brearley.

de Geus was Royal Dutch Shell's strategy director – he talks about the need to constantly revalidate where you are going in the light of the inevitability of external environmental changes.

Espejo, R., et al. (1996). *Organisational Transformation and Learning*. Chichester, John Wiley & Sons.

An easier introduction than some of the others, talking about cybernetic theory as applied to management – I emphasise 'easier'. Didn't say 'easy', though.

Flyvbjerg, B. (2003). *Megaprojects and Risk*. Cambridge, Cambridge University Press.

Some excellent case examples of the issues in managing complex projects.

Gardener, T. M. J. (2008). "Changing Behaviours in Defence Acquisition: A Game Theory Approach." *Journal of the Operational Research Society* **59**: 225–230.

Don't necessarily agree with this, but it's worth thinking about.

Gray, B. (8 December 2009). You Can Have Good Services and Save Cash. *The Times*. London.

Article that accompanied the publication of the paper on defence spending.

Handy, C. (1996). *Beyond Certainty*. London, Arrow.

To uncertainty… and beyond! Charles Handy is very readable, yet the points he make are serious indeed. A strong argument for the need for Second Order thinking.

Hass, K. (2009). *Managing Complex Projects – A New Model*. Vienna, VA, Management Concepts.

Personally, I struggled to find anything new at all in this. It's also quite prescriptive – at the level of motherhood and apple pie. I include it in this list reluctantly, and only as a warning against easy, instant solutions to Complex Project Management.

Hoggart, R. (1992 [Reprint]). *The Uses of Literacy*. London, Penguin.

Because the wider we read, the broader our repertoire. In my opinion, every engineer and project manager should be made to read and review at least three novels a year to maintain their registration.

Introna, L. D. (1997). *Management, Information and Power*. Basingstoke, Macmillan.

Although this is one of the worst edited books I have ever read, once you get behind the bad grammar, convoluted and often unconcluded arguments, there are some stimulating ideas here.

Jackson, M. C. (2003) *Systems Thinking*. Chichester, John Wiley & Sons

An excellent introduction to the various tools and techniques in the Systems Thinking discipline.

Kegan, R. and Lahey, L. L. (2001). "The Real Reason People Won't Change." *Harvard Business Review* (November): 85–92.

Kegan and Lahey come from a business psychology background, and their understanding of what *really* motivates people at work is informed, erudite and in my view borne out in my own experience.

Kolb, D. A. (1984). *Experiential Learning*. New Jersey, Prentice Hall.

This is the book that first defined the learning cycle.

Macneil, I. R (1978 [2nd Ed.]). *Contracts: Exchange Transactions and Relations*. Mineola, Foundation Press (1st Edn, 1971).

I'm no finance man, but the arguments are clear and (to me) persuasive.

Mitroff, I. I. and Linstone, H. A. (1993). *The Unbounded Mind*. Oxford, OUP.

I know this is in the bibliography, but it's so good I've put it here as well.

Remington, K. and Pollack, J. (2007). *Tools for Complex Projects*. Aldershot, Gower.

Does exactly what it says on the tin, and succeeds in doing everything the Hass book attempts to do and fails. After you've read my book, this should be the next on your reading list. If you can't afford both, if I were you, I'd go for this!

Schein, E. (1987) *The Clinical Perspective in Fieldwork*. Beverly Hills, CA, Sage.

Edgar Schein presents an academically valid research methodology for practitioners who aren't in a position to observe from a detached position. An ideal approach for Learning both in- and from-experience.

Simon, H. A. (1983). *Reason in Human Affairs*. Stanford, CA, Stanford University Press.

How people really make decisions – the concept of 'Bounded rationality'.

Solomon, R. C. and Flores, F. (2001). *Building Trust.* Oxford, OUP.

Trust as an 'emotional skill' which can never be earned, only awarded. In talking to people about Complex Projects, the word 'trust' is the one you hear most frequently – usually in the negative – *"We can't trust them"*.

Stacey, R.D. et al. (2000). *Complexity and Management.* London, Routledge.

Suggests that Systems Thinking isn't the Philosopher's Stone in Complexity Management – it's more about human beings, their relationships and behaviours. Doing things differently means that we have to address those behaviours.

Williamson, O. E. (2002). "The Theory of the Firm as Governance Structure: From Choice to Contract." *Journal of Economic Perspectives* **16**(3): 171–195.

A possible way forward for appropriate contracting.

Winograd, T. and F. Flores (1987). *Understanding Computers and Cognition.* New Jersey, Addison-Wesley.

Ground-breaking and fascinating. The 'Computers' bit is way out of date, but the 'Cognition' chapters are still spot on.

INDEX

user, need for involvement 34

values 88–9
variety, requisite variety 43
Viable Systems Model (VSM) 44,
   98–9

vision 19–21, 88

Weltanschauung 34, 106
wisdom 49–51, 65

ADVANCES IN PROJECT MANAGEMENT

Advances in Project Management provides short, state of play guides to the main aspects of the new emerging applications, including: maturity models, agile projects, extreme projects, Six Sigma and projects, human factors and leadership in projects, project governance, value management, virtual teams and project benefits.

CURRENTLY PUBLISHED TITLES

Managing Project Uncertainty, David Cleden 978-0-566-08840-7

Strategic Project Risk Appraisal and Management, Elaine Harris 978-0-566-08848-3

Project-Oriented Leadership, Ralf Müller and J. Rodney Turner 978-0-566-08923-7

Tame, Messy and Wicked Risk Leadership, David Hancock 978-0-566-09242-8

Managing Project Supply Chains, Ron Basu 978-1-4094-2515-1

REVIEWS OF THE SERIES

Managing Project Uncertainty, David Cleden

> *This is a must-read book for anyone involved in project management. The author's carefully crafted work meets all my "4Cs" review criteria. The book is clear, cogent, concise*

and complete ... it is a brave author who essays to write about managing project uncertainty in a text extending to only 117 pages (soft-cover version). In my opinion, David Cleden succeeds brilliantly. ... For project managers this book, far from being a short-lived stress anodyne, will provide a confidence-boosting tonic. Project uncertainty? Bring it on, I say!

International Journal of Managing Projects in Business

Uncertainty is an inevitable aspect of most projects, but even the most proficient project manager struggles to successfully contain it. Many projects overrun and consume more funds than were originally budgeted, often leading to unplanned expense and outright programme failure. David examines how uncertainty occurs and provides management strategies that the user can put to immediate use on their own project work. He also provides a series of pre-emptive uncertainty and risk avoidance strategies that should be the cornerstone of any planning exercise for all personnel involved in project work.

I have been delivering both large and small projects and programmes in the public and private sector since 1989. I wish this book had been available when I began my career in project work. I strongly commend this book to all project professionals.

Lee Hendricks, Sales & Marketing Director,
SunGard Public Sector

The book under review is an excellent presentation of a comprehensive set of explorations about uncertainty (its recognition) in the context of projects. It does a good job of all along reinforcing the difference between risk (known unknowns) management and managing uncertainty (unknown unknowns – "bolt from the blue"). The author lucidly presents a variety of frameworks/models so that the reader easily grasps the varied forms in which uncertainty presents itself in the context of projects.

VISION: The Journal of Business Perspective (India)

Cleden will leave you with a sound understanding about the traits, tendencies, timing and tenacity of uncertainty in projects. He is also adept at identifying certain methods that try to contain the uncertainty, and why some prove more successful than others. Those who expect risk management to be the be-all, end-all for uncertainty solutions will be in for a rude awakening.

Brad Egeland, Project Management Tips

Strategic Project Risk Appraisal and Management, Elaine Harris

Elaine Harris's volume is timely. In a world of books by "instant experts" it's pleasing to read something by someone who clearly knows their onions, and has a passion for the subject. In summary, this is a thorough and engaging book.
Chris Morgan, Head of Business Assurance for Select Plant Hire,
Quality World

As soon as I met Elaine I realised that we both shared a passion to better understand the inherent risk in any project, be that capital investment, expansion capital or expansion of assets. What is seldom analysed are the components of knowledge necessary to make a good judgement, the impact of our own prejudices in relation to projects or for that matter the cultural elements within an organisation which impact upon the decision making process. Elaine created a system to break this down and give reasons and logic to both the process and the human interaction necessary to improve the chances of success. Adopting her recommendations will improve teamwork and outcomes for your company.
Edward Roderick Hon. LLD, former CEO Christian Salvesen plc

Tame, Messy and Wicked Risk Leadership, David Hancock

This book takes project risk management firmly onto a higher and wider plane. We thought we knew what project risk management was and what it could do. David Hancock shows us a great deal more of both. David Hancock has probably read more about risk management than almost anybody else; he has almost certainly thought about it as much as anybody else and he has quite certainly learnt from doing it on very difficult projects as much as anybody else. His book draws fully on all three components. For a book which tackles a complex subject with breadth, insight and novelty – it's remarkable that it is also a really good read. I could go on!

Dr Martin Barnes CBE FREng, President, The Association for
Project Management

This compact and thought-provoking description of risk management will be useful to anybody with responsibilities for projects, programmes or businesses. It hits the nail on the head in so many ways, for example by pointing out that risk management can easily drift into a checklist mindset, driven by the production of registers of numerous occurrences characterised by the Risk = Probablity × Consequence equation. David Hancock points out that real life is much more complicated, with the heart of the problem lying in people, so that real life resembles poker rather than roulette. He also points out that while the important thing is to solve the right problem, many real-life issues cannot be readily described in a definitive statement of the problem. There are often interrelated individual problems with surrounding social issues and he describes these real-life situations as "Wicked Messes". Unusual terminology, but definitely worth the read, as much for the overall problem description as for the recommended strategies for getting to grips with real-life risk management. I have no hesitation in recommending this book.

Sir Robert Walmsley KCB FREng, Chairman of the Board of the
Major Projects Association

In highlighting the complexity of many of today's problems and defining them as tame, messy or wicked, David Hancock brings a new perspective to the risk issues that we currently face. He challenges risk managers, and particularly those involved in project risk management, to take a much broader approach to the assessment of risk and consider the social, political and behavioural dimensions of each problem, as well as the scientific and engineering aspects with which they are most comfortable. In this way, risks will be viewed more holistically and managed more effectively than at present.

Dr Lynn T. Drennan, Chief Executive Alarm,
The Public Risk Management Association

ABOUT THE EDITOR

Professor Darren Dalcher is founder and Director of the National Centre for Project Management, a Professor of Software Project Management at Middlesex University and Visiting Professor of Computer Science at the University of Iceland. Professor Dalcher has been named by the Association for Project Management as one of the top 10 'movers and shapers' in project management. He has also been voted *Project Magazine*'s Academic of the Year for his contribution in 'integrating and weaving academic work with practice'.

Professor Dalcher is active in numerous international committees, steering groups and editorial boards. He is heavily involved in organising international conferences, and has delivered many keynote addresses and tutorials. He has written over 150 papers and book chapters on project management and software engineering. He is Editor-in-Chief of *Software Process Improvement and Practice*, an international journal focusing on capability, maturity, growth and improvement.

Professor Dalcher is a Fellow of the Association for Project Management and the British Computer Society, and a Member of the Project Management Institute, the Academy of Management, the Institute for Electrical and Electronics Engineers and the Association for Computing Machinery. He is a Chartered IT Practitioner. He is a member of the PMI Advisory Board responsible for the prestigious David I. Cleland project management award, and of the APM Professional Development Board.

National Centre for Project Management
Middlesex University
College House
Trent Park
Bramley Road
London N14 4YZ
Email: ncpm@mdx.ac.uk
Phone: +44 (0)20 8411 2299